The UFO Deception

Also by Father Spyridon

Journey To Mount Athos
The Ancient Path
Trampling Down Death By Death
Fire On The Lips
Vampire AD70
Return To Mount Athos
Small Steps Into The Kingdom
Lost Voices
Out Of Order
Podvig
Orthodoxy And The Kingdom of Satan
Come And See
Behind The Veil
In Search Of Holy Russia

The UFO Deception

An Orthodox Christian Perspective

Father Spyridon Bailey

Published in 2021 by FeedARead.com Publishing
Funded by the Arts Council of Great Britain

A CIP catalogue record for this title is available from
the British Library.

To Stephanie

Contents

The original newspaper cutting kept by Father Spyridon's wife appears on p.13

Chapter One – A Reliable Witness

On New Year's Eve in 1978, a couple were driving with their thirteen year old daughter to a family party in Rotherham in the North of England. They were heading from the outskirts of Sheffield along a stretch of road where there wasn't much housing. It was still early evening but the December sky had already turned dark black; the lack of light from buildings or street lights only added to the darkness of the night. As they travelled down a long, straight stretch of road bordered by fields on either side, they saw something ahead of them in the distance. The young girl, who is now fifty-six in 2021, takes up the story.

"We first saw a golden light ahead of us, my dad made a joke about it looking like a UFO, and we all laughed. As we continued driving we all watched it getting closer, and my dad slowed down so he could focus on it. As the light slowly moved towards us we pulled in to a lay-by at the side of the road, all of us now very quiet. It kept coming in our direction until it was about twenty metres away over the hedge of the field from us, and once it came alongside it stopped moving and hovered where it was. I couldn't believe how big it was, bigger than a double decker bus, it just hung silently next to us. It was shaped like a cigar, a golden cigar without any windows or seams, completely smooth, but you could tell it was solid. As it had moved it left a long, golden trail behind it that stretched back along where it had been. Even though it was golden, it didn't look ghostly, it looked like a real object. I remember looking back and forth at my mom and dad, I had to confirm to myself they were looking at the same thing I was seeing; if I had been by myself I would have doubted I had seen it or thought I had hallucinated it, it was just so incredible. They were obviously looking at the same thing in the sky, their mouths were open and they just stared at it in silence. In the end I had to ask them if they were seeing the cigar-shaped object I could see and they nodded without saying a word. After a few seconds my dad reached for the door handle to get out of the car but I asked him to stay with us, which he did.

A few more seconds passed before the object slowly and silently began to pull away from us and followed an arc over the field. It then began to speed up and pulled away very fast and I remember being amazed at how its height above the ground didn't change, like it was following an exact path or plain. We didn't really feel fear or anything special, there was just an enormous sense of surprise at seeing something so strange that we couldn't understand. I remember knowing it was like nothing people could make, it was beyond the technology of our time. It didn't make us emotional in any way, and all these years later I can say it never affected me in any way. I was never interested in that kind of thing, and seeing this didn't make me want to find out about them, it just always struck me as an odd event.

As it pulled away we realised that another car had pulled in behind us, but once the object was gone we didn't get out to speak to them, my dad just pulled out into the road and we headed to the party. When we arrived my mom ran in telling everyone we had seen a UFO, and they all laughed at her. For the whole night we were the butt of every body's jokes and my dad never mentioned it again. Two days later it was in the newspapers that these things had been seen up and down the country, and I remember when the new term started going back to school and telling everyone about it and they all mocked me terribly, so I never mentioned it again. I kept quiet about it for the next forty years, but I kept a newspaper cutting in a box of things."

I begin this book with this account, which is so like countless other experiences described by witnesses of UFOs, because it comes from my wife. We hear stories of strange experiences, and often we are suspicious, we question the honesty of the story teller, we may even wonder about their sanity. I have shared in this kind of scepticism and looked for explanations to brush such claims aside. But faced with someone I have absolute trust in, I am confronted with the realisation that there is indeed a genuine experience behind these accounts. Having a witness I can believe is enough to convince me, but for other people my wife's testimony is just one more familiar claim to something unexplainable. Therefore more evidence is needed which I will try to provide.

I had been reading *Orthodoxy And The Religion Of The Future* by Father Seraphim Rose, which had prompted my wife to tell me of her experience and dig out the old newspaper cutting (which can be seen below). In it the reporter describes how "Thousands of people reported seeing space ships in the skies on New Year's Eve." He goes on to say that "UFO sightings came from as far apart as Cornwall and the Scottish Highlands." Witnesses reported seeing huge ships as well as sightings of the cigar shaped object seen by my wife and her family. Other details such as the long vapour trail mentioned by my wife were described by many people. Father Seraphim was writing in the 1970s, and his treatment of the topic came as a chapter in a book covering a number of subjects. With the release of official documents by the U.K. government and footage claimed to be of UFOs by the U.S. Navy, I decided in 2020 to read further and attempt to understand what lies behind the phenomenon. As I researched the topic I became more convinced of the accuracy of Father Seraphim Rose's interpretation of the events, and decided a more thorough presentation was needed.

The material covering this topic is almost endless: articles, websites, books and now documentaries and whole series of television programmes are produced on it. On any single day there are at least two programmes about UFOs or aliens as part of SKY TV's output in the U.K.. But with few exceptions, the Orthodox Christian perspective is missing, and so conclusions are reached based on materialistic, occult or heretical thinking. But in fact there is a wealth of writing from the Church to support us in our understanding of this phenomenon, and also how we should respond to it. I am fully aware that for many devotees of the myth of aliens, the perspective here will be uncomfortable. However, the evidence is strong for arguing that there are two phenomena taking place in parallel, and that those behind each are using the other as a mask for their activities. It is a very real deception, carried out by those who need to conceal their actions from us. There is a great deal of confusion created by this, particularly among those who wish to explain all UFO sightings and encounters as either one thing or the other: I will attempt to demonstrate that this approach is flawed and only leaves us vulnerable to the deception.

So let us return to the issue of a reliable witness. As I have said, I have certainty that there is something real happening, that we aren't only dealing with liars or those looking for attention, though this may be the case on some or many occasions. I have the testimony of my wife. So my first objective, before looking at the details of the phenomenon, its characteristics, effects and dangers, is to present evidence that will convince you that we are talking about something that cannot be rejected as fantasy. We will then consider the changing nature of the phenomenon through recent history, and how the philosophies and cultural assumptions of different times have shaped the interpretation of what is happening. We will also observe how the phenomenon is being used by military agencies and how the idea of ETs has proved convenient for them. But I hope too to convince you that the modern story of aliens visiting us from other planets is worse than a myth: it is a deception.

DAILY EXPRESS Tuesday January 2 1975

OVER BRITAIN UFO reports flood in

RIDDLE

'It was like an orange cigar with a three mile vapour trail'

Sir Bernard Lovell

THOUSANDS of people reported seeing " space ships " in the sky on New Year's Eve.

UFO sightings came from as far apart as Cornwall and the Scottish Highlands. Descriptions tallied in many instances and UFO Association officials were impressed by the quality of the reports.

Flying saucers were reported as well as giant planes, three-mile-long rocket ships and cigar-shaped objects travelling at 5,000 miles an hour.

Calls were received by the Ministry of Defence, police and R.A.F., from doctors, policemen, social workers and an astrologer.

Sober

All the sightings are being investigated. A senior police officer said : "It should be made clear that these reports came from very sober, very responsible people.

"Police officers on duty put in reports as well as the public.

At Manchester Airport, a spokesman said : "We had a deluge of calls at around 7.30 on New Year's Eve.

We had calls from the Lake

By Trevor Reynolds

District and Hull and from people who claimed they had spotted UFOs near the airport. We have logged all the incidents."

At his mountain home in Wales, 38-year-old Chris Turner, who has a view of 60 miles from his lounge, said : "I have been studying the sky for 30 years.

"What I saw I have estimated as about 50 miles away. It had a three-mile vapour trail and an estimated speed of 4,680 miles an hour. It was like an orange cigar."

A similar object was reported in Hull, Cornwall and Boston, Lines.

Social worker Paul Clegg,

28, and four friends saw it from a Manchester suburb.

Dr. John Rees, 38, was driving along the M56 when he saw what looked like a plane on fire with a long vapour trail.

A cigar-shaped object with a big vapour trail was reported by Cheshire surgeon Mr. Harold Hassall.

"It moved in a straight line with no noise. It defied any orthodox analysis," he said.

Mr. Hassall's neighbour a sandwich builder Mr. Don Cartwright, saw portholes aflame with incandescence.

Strange

Solicitor's son Mark Henderson, 15, of Bradwell Sandbach, followed the trail of the slowly-moving object on his motorcycle.

"When it hovered, a strange light illuminated the countryside," he said.

"It looked as if it might come so I headed back for home."

The Ministry of Defence said the mystery objects were probably space debris—satellites burning up on re-entering the earth's atmosphere.

A spokesman for Sir Bernard Lovell, head of Jodrell Bank, said : "The sightings would appear to be space debris but we are really not sure at this stage.

"The weather has been very clear. One would be able to see meteorites with the naked

13

Chapter Two – The Period Of Modern Sightings

The evidence that something is being seen in the skies by reliable witnesses is overwhelming. For nearly eighty years (what is often described as the period of modern sightings) eye-witnesses have been giving accounts of their experiences which include very similar details. As a result of freedom of information applications and subsequent government admissions, there have been at least two major military investigations in the United States since 1945, and a similarly large one conducted by the French government. The results of these investigations have not been fully disclosed, and as we shall see, there is a great deal of evidence that suggests that the UFO phenomenon is paranormal in nature, and beyond the expertise of those examining it.

The official story about UFOs began in 1933 when sightings were reported in Scandinavian newspapers of what were called "ghost ships". In the same year there were some sightings too in Britain, and eye-witnesses described strange aircraft circling low over the ground, often in poor flying conditions, emitting powerful beams of light as though searching for something. The result was that on 28th December 1933 the 4th Swedish Flying Corps started an investigation to find out what was happening in their airspace. In the following year Major-General Reuterswaerd issued a statement to the Swedish press in which he stated

There are many reports from reliable
people which describe close observations of
the enigmatic flier. The question is who or
whom are they, and why are they invading our
air territory?(1)

Despite the efforts of the Swedish military, the mystery was never solved. On 1st February 1934 The Times newspaper reported that one of these objects had been flying over London for two hours with many witnesses. Such was the seriousness of the event that four days later the Under-Secretary of State for Air, Sir Philip Sassoon, was forced to make a statement about it in the House of Commons, claiming that it must have been a Royal Airforce craft, despite the RAF being forbidden to fly at less than five thousand feet over London. Also, the sightings often took place in conditions which would have been extremely treacherous for aeroplanes to fly in.

On 25th February 1942 there occurred a sighting of something over Los Angeles that resulted in nearly fifteen hundred rounds of anti-aircraft shells being fired into the sky from ground forces. This was just three months after the attack on Pearl Harbour and many people were still jumpy. Air raid sirens were set off and the city shut out its lights. No U.S. Airforce aeroplanes were sent to intercept the attack, and according to the Herald Express many thousands of people watched the shells exploding without effect on whatever hovered over the city. Eventually the object flew slowly down the coast, taking twenty minutes to cover twenty miles before witnesses said it disappeared. The subsequent investigation sent a report to President Franklin Roosevelt that said the sightings must have been of some kind of aircraft but could not explain how or why it had not been brought down by the shelling. The event is said to have caused great panic amongst the L.A. population and a number of people were reported to have died from heart-attacks.

During the Second World War there were many reports from Allied aircrews of small, spherical objects that flew around them as they made their bombing runs. The bulk of sightings occurred from 1943 to 1944 and were so common that crews nicknamed the objects Foo Fighters. The possibility that the Germans had developed a new technology was taken seriously by military officials, and in 1943 Lieutenant-General Massey led a British team to investigate what the pilots were witnessing. It was concluded that since no harm or interference with the Allied aeroplanes was taking place, they must be some form of psychological operation. Massey eventually realised that the German crews were experiencing the same encounters and that the Germans had themselves set up an investigation. The small objects behaved as though their movement was being controlled, coming close to aircraft, flying alongside and then departing at great speed.

In 1946 there were thousands of reported sightings of what were called "ghost rockets" in Finland, Norway, Sweden and Denmark. The sightings then spread to many other countries including Greece and Italy. The objects were described as being rocket shaped and making manoeuvres no known aircraft could accomplish. Cases were particularly common in Sweden again, which led to the U.S. Embassy there sending a telegram on 11th July 1946 which stated

For some weeks there have been
numerous reports of strange rocket-like
missiles being seen in Swedish and Finnish
skies. One landed on a beach near
Stockholm without causing any damage and
according to press, fragments are now
being studied by military authorities.
Local scientists on first inspection stated
it contained organic substance. Missiles
observed made no sound and seemed to be
falling rapidly to earth. No sound of
explosion followed however. Swedes
profess ignorance to origin.

The Swedish General Staff described the situation as extremely dangerous and there were public statements made that suggested the Soviets must have been testing some new weapon.(2) Sweden requested assistance from Britain and the United States to deal with what was happening, but still no explanation could be found. Eventually the

Norwegian General Staff instructed all Norwegian newspapers to stop reporting on what was happening in the hope of reducing public anxiety.(3) On the 6th September 1946 the Daily Telegraph published a photograph of one of the objects which showed that the entity was within the flame trail rather than at the head of it, leading Swedish authorities to conclude that it was an unknown form of technology. Even dismissing many sightings as natural phenomena, the Swedes admitted that over two hundred of the objects had been tracked on radar.

In the same year on 5th September, the Greek Prime Minister Tsaldaris publicly acknowledged that many objects had been seen in the skies over Macedonia and Salonika (4) and a team of Greek scientists was tasked with explaining them. The leader of the investigation was the respected engineer Professor Paul Santorini (designer of the fuse for the atomic bomb that was dropped on Hiroshima). On the 24th February 1967 Santorini addressed the Greek Astronautical Society and said of the investigation

We soon established that they were not
missiles. But before we could do any more,
the Army, after conferring with foreign
officials, ordered the investigation
stopped. Foreign scientists flew
into Greece for secret talks with me. (5)

When the UFO researcher Raymond Fowler contacted Professor Santini to confirm the newspaper reports that he had made this statement,

Santini not only confirmed it but added that he believed that "a world blanket of secrecy surrounded the UFO question."(6)

One of the most famous incidents in UFO history was the one that took place in Roswell, New Mexico in 1947. On 2nd July numerous witnesses claimed to have seen a bright disc in the sky heading north-west. Witnesses claim that the object crashed about seventy-five miles north of Roswell, where a rancher named William Brazel, with his son and daughter, found the wreckage. The case has always raised suspicions about government involvement because of what happened when Brazel contacted the authorities. Major Jesse Marcel, a staff intelligence office of the 509th Bomb Group Intelligence Office at Roswell Field Airforce base was sent to recover what could be found, and the base issued a statement under the authority of its commanding officer, Colonel William Blanchard, which said that wreckage from a flying disc had been located. Orders were given to fly everything that had been recovered on a B-29 to Wright Field in Dayton, Ohio, for further examination. General Roger Ramey quickly took charge of the operation and ordered everyone involved to give no further information to reporters. While a second statement was being issued to the press which claimed that the wreckage was nothing more than a weather balloon, the crash site was stripped of every fragment that could be found and everything was kept under armed guard at Wright Field. Major Marcel was shut away for a week following the incident, but later said that one piece of the wreckage could not be bent or marked even with hammers.(7) Marcel was a pilot with 468 hours of combat flying with multiple medals for shooting down German aeroplanes during the Second World War; and yet it was now being claimed that he couldn't distinguish between a weather balloon and a crashed disc. He went on to achieve the rank of Lieutenant Colonel and was assigned to a special weapons programme, suggesting that his integrity was not questioned by his superiors. Despite claims from others that there was a second crash site and that bodies were found there, Marcel always dismissed this and said he saw no evidence of any of this.

One of those intrigued by the Roswell incident was the nuclear physicist Stanton Friedman who went on to interview ninety-two people involved with the supposed crash, thirty of whom claimed to be direct witnesses. The story consumed Friedman who has gone on to write and debate the UFO phenomenon to this day, and has dedicated his website to the exposure of what he considers the truth of what is happening. Ten of Friedman's interviewees claimed the Roswell object was non-terrestrial, and many have argued that a government cover-up is taking place.(8)

UFO sightings often come in waves such as in 1952 when there were so many that briefings were sent from the Armed Forces Security Agencies (a version of the National Security Agency in its day) to the Joint Chiefs of Staff and the CIA.(9) The sightings reached a peak when on 19th July UFOs were seen over Washington DC by many airline crews and the objects were tracked on radar at Air Traffic Control at Washington National Airport. Pilots described seeing the objects cruising at around a hundred miles per hour before disappearing at incredible speeds. In 1985 a USAF intelligence report was finally released concerning the appearance of UFOs over Washington on 26th July 1952. It states:

Varying numbers (up to 12 simultaneously) of unidentified targets on Air Traffic Control Center, Washington National Airport radar scope. Radar operators said there could have been other unidentified targets on their scopes outside their area of control. All ARTC crew members were emphatic that the unidentified returns were solid. Unidentified returns have been picked up from time to time over the last few months, but never in such quantities over such a prolonged period.(10)

Further waves continued to arrive, such as in 1965 when U.S. Naval and Air attaches reported that newspapers were describing many sightings in South America. Attaches also reported on direct sightings by aircrew, such as the pilots of Chilean National Airlines Flight LAN 904 on 6th September. The captain of the flight, Marcelo Cisternas, watched it for nearly a quarter of an hour, claiming that it was constantly emitting intense changing colours.

Such series of multiple sightings have continued, as in Brazil in 1973 and again in 1986, when the Brazillian Defence Centre went to its highest level of alert when radars were filled with unidentified objects that were causing major disruption to ordinary air traffic. Three Tiger Jets were sent from Sao Paulo and reported chasing glowing objects that kept changing colours, but were too quick to intercept. The President of Brazil, Jose Sarney, decided to release news of the sightings to the public, and Air Minister Brigadier Otavio Julio Moreira Lima assured reporters at a press conference that Brazilian radar had not malfunctioned, and that whatever had been detected was real.

Waves of sightings have occurred in such numbers around the world that it would take up too much space to list them here.(11) Observers have begun to notice patterns of where sightings take place, such as the large number around Puerto Rico since 1987, and as a result, all kinds of fanciful theories have developed, ranging from underground alien bases, to theories about lay-lines and the various energy fields that surround the earth. As we shall see, this is one of the key dangers in the subject of UFOs. Unanswered questions leave people filling the gaps with whatever their imagination can create, and as people's involvement grows, their fantasies can become more dangerous.

Before considering how governments have responded to the sightings, there are two specific cases we should include. The first occurred at Rendlesham Forest, in Suffolk, England in 1980. Colonel Charles Halt was deputy-commander of a U.S. unit based at RAF Bentwaters and on 26th December Airforce security reported sightings of strange lights. Halt has since gathered testimonies from RAF radar operators at Bentwaters and nearby Wattisham airfield confirming that they tracked an unidentified object that night. At around three in the morning, the security patrol reported seeing strange lights descending into the forest. Thinking an aircraft might have crashed, the officers investigated the site and found a glowing metallic object. One of the men, Sergeant Jim Penniston said that as they tried to approach the object it lifted away from them through the trees, causing local farm animals to go into a frenzy. Penniston reported the object as being "a craft of unknown origin". The following day men were sent out from the base and found three small marks in the ground where the object had been. They also reported finding branches of trees burned and broken along the trajectory of the object. Colonel Halt then led a group of servicemen to make further observations, during which he made a live recording on a cassette recorder. While they investigated, they saw three bright lights which hovered above them for two or three hours, and seemed to beam down lights to the earth.

The case has gathered attention because under The Freedom Of Information Act in 1983, access was given to a memorandum sent by Halt to the

Ministry of Defence describing what he and his men had seen, leading to a front page story in The News of the World. In 1984 a copy of the recording made by Halt on the night was released to UFO researchers by Colonel Sam Morgan who had taken over as the U.S. senior officer on the base. In June 2010, Halt signed a notarised affidavit claiming the event he had witnessed was extra-terrestrial and that both the U.K. and U.S. governments were deceiving their citizens over UFOs. It was later discovered that though the U.K. Ministry of Defence publicly dismissed the story, they had in fact kept a large file on the incident and were clearly far more interested or concerned than they had admitted. As awareness of the story has grown, so too have the number of attempts to debunk it, including personal attacks on Colonel Halt and dismissive accounts on the BBC. Despite the front page coverage in the *News of the World*, many of the airmen have stayed silent about the incident out of concern for their careers. Since they are all now past retirement age some have begun to tell their stories. Colonel Halt has recorded their accounts and taken his evidence to promote the story in public presentations.

The case of Commander David Fravor has received a lot of attention as a result of the naval officer giving a number of interviews throughout 2019. Commander Fravor's story has a lot of credibility because of his background and experience: he flew for eighteen years in the U.S. Navy, was awarded every military flying qualification possible, and became commanding officer of the Black Aces.(12) Unlike many accounts, Commander Fravor's experience was captured on the jet's targeting recorder by one of his crew.

On 14th November 2004, his squadron was flying off the coast of Mexico in a training exercise involving an aircraft carrier as well as a number of support ships. What Commander Fravor was not told was that for the previous two weeks the USS Princeton had been tracking unidentified objects dropping from the sky into that area. Up to a dozen objects were coming down from about eighty thousand feet to twenty thousand feet, where they would remain for a few hours before climbing vertically at speeds no known vehicle could achieve. In fact, describing them as coming down from this height is a little misleading, since this is simply the maximum height they could be tracked at: Fravor and the other men involved believed that the objects were coming from beyond the Earth's atmosphere.

At around noon Commander Fravor was about to engage in the planned exercise when he was contacted to abort on the grounds that he had to investigate the presence of something beyond the flight area of the exercise. As they flew out to sea, Fravor was informed for the first time of the radar sightings of the unidentified objects which he was now being instructed to examine.

As they approached the target Fravor recalls how calm the sea looked except for white water where there was something disrupting the surface. He describes it as looking like a cross shape that was around the size of a 737 jet (around forty metres long and thirty-five metres wide). As this drew his attention he noticed a cigar or tic-tac shaped object that was around twelve metres in length which was just above the surface of the water. The pilot of one of the other jets confirmed over the radio seeing the same thing. The object was moving back and forth along the lines of the shape under the water, but was creating no disturbance in the water beneath it. Commander Fravor describes its movements as looking like a ping pong ball bouncing back and forth.

Fravor left the other jet that was accompanying him at twenty thousand feet and flew down to take a closer look. As he slowly descended, the object changed direction and began to ascend. His impression was that it was reacting to his own jet's presence and seemed to turn towards him. As he circled just two thousand feet above it, Fravor decided to turn directly towards it to see how close he could get to it; he was within half a mile of it when, within a second the object vanished. The jet above him confirmed that it had vanished from their view too. Commander Fravor then turned back to investigate whatever was beneath the water but discovered that this had also disappeared.

After reporting what had happened the squadron headed back towards the east, when the radar on the U.S.S. Princeton informed Fravor that the object had reappeared back along their original flight path. It had travelled approximately sixty miles in thirty seconds. The radar operator confirmed that he hadn't tracked the object moving to its new location, it had simply appeared there. The squadron made two sweeps of the area without finding the object and so returned to the aircraft carrier. News of what had happened had spread amongst the ship's crew, and as a Super Hornet was about to take off, the pilot insisted he would use his more sensitive tracking equipment to try and find it. The Super Hornet is able to identify a point on the radar and focus its different sensors on that object, which allows different forms of filming to be synchronised.

As the two man crew flew out they located the UFO, but as the weapons operator tried to lock the radar in on it, they found their radar being jammed. This was not a malfunction in the jet's equipment, they were able to determine that some form of radar disablement was being used on them. The weapons operator immediately switched to his targeting equipment and was able to video the object as it hovered. The video is now available on the internet and shows the flight information as well as the object being observed. In the infra-red mode, the footage shows that there was no heat plume, which means it was not using any conventional means of propulsion (a jet engine creates a hot plume of gas). Even in black and white TV mode, the video shows no kind of exhaust coming from it. All the time the radar was unable to identify the range of the object, meaning it continued using some means to actively jam the jet's equipment. As the jet continued to approach, the object suddenly shot out of the camera's view, at a speed Commander Fravor describes as being beyond anything our technology is capable of. Even as it sped away, the object created no exhaust trail. With the ability to observe an aircraft up to fifty miles away, it is remarkable that within a second the object could no longer be seen.

Commander Fravor says the story was never classified in any way. None of the aircrew were instructed to remain silent, and the video footage was never confiscated. All crew and tapes were subjected to a debriefing, and the video was copied and archived by the Navy. Fravor admits that interest in the event has meant that for most people his entire flying career, consisting of over five thousand hours in the air, has been reduced to that five minutes off the coast of Mexico. He has since talked to other pilots who have witnessed similar objects and has discovered that off the east coast of America the sightings are quite common. There are even accounts of aeroplanes nearly colliding with the objects. Consequently, when radar operators spot them, a warning notice is issued to pilots flying in the area.

Commander Fravor presents a story that is supported by multiple radar operators as well as a number of pilots and weapon operators. Therefore it is clear that this is not the result of a problem with technology or a single eye witness lying or being mistaken. He says he has been invited twice to Washington DC to talk about his experience with what he will only describe as high level government officials. The other pilot involved in the incident has been summoned to the Pentagon numerous times and claims to have bene asked to compare her sighting with what other pilots have reported. As a result of the exposure the "Tic Tac" incident has received, it has been revealed that the United States Government has been running a classified programme called the Advanced Aerospace Threat Identification Program (AATIP). The programme was set up to study unexplained aerial phenomena (UAP), with a particular reference to sightings by military personnel. The twenty-two million dollars spent on this project came to public awareness in 2017, when the US government claimed that it had only been in operation for five years and had come to an end in 2012. As many people suspected, intelligence agencies continued to be interested in the subject and in a 2020 Senate hearing of the United States Senate Select Committee on Intelligence, it was disclosed that The Unidentified Aerial Phenomena Task Force (UAPTF) is currently operating. This is run within the Office of Naval Intelligence and gathers information on what it calls unexplained aerial vehicles.

The effect on Fravor has been to lead him to look at the history of technology and wonder whether many of our beliefs about what is possible are based on false assumptions. He says "If something can appear anywhere at will and do what it wants, we better give it our attention."(13)

This story raises different questions. The fact that Commander Fravor is a high ranking military officer means different things to different people, depending on the presuppositions they already have. It is argued that with his training, Fravor provides a reliable witness report. While his background suggests the exact opposite to other people, who argue that sightings from military personnel cannot be trusted because any such statements would be tightly controlled by the intelligence agencies, and anything he says could be part of a system of disinformation. This is one of the central difficulties with the whole subject: since there are so few hard facts that do not need some kind of interpretation, all conclusions will be highly subjective and dependant on opinion or intent.

The "Tic-Tac" incident was part of a wider release of information that received front page coverage in the New York Times in December 2017. This was just one of a dozen stories that has now appeared in the Times over recent years. While the Pentagon has officially acknowledged the existence of UAPTF and the possibility of unknown aircraft flying in and around US airspace, it appears that there is no great concern about it amongst government or military officials, and the news gained little reaction from the general public. Reports on ABC News and CNN picked up on the story, and Brett Baier on Fox News claimed "A lot of people are taking this revelation seriously," but beyond the groups already captivated by UFOs, it seems the news made little impact on anyone. The New York Times stated in its article that the previous director of UAPTF was "convinced that objects of undetermined origin have crashed on earth with materials retrieved for study," and that these materials retrieved were now in the hands of both military and private groups. The Times quoted astrophysicist Eric Davis, who worked as a consultant for the program, as saying of the materials "we couldn't make it ourselves." Davis went further and said that he briefed the Defense Department in March 2017 regarding retrievals from "off-world vehicles not made on this earth."

It is interesting that the release of stories and information about UFOs has led the public to a point where the New York Times can quote someone making these kinds of statements and there are no major consequences. Politicians didn't demand answers, people continued to turn up for work the following day, and a level of acceptance and normality had been established about the possibility of aliens visiting the earth. Meanwhile, those who are suspicious of any information coming from the military question the motives for presenting the story while at the same time appearing to do very little about it. We will now consider the reaction of various governments to these kinds of events and use them to reinforce the case that there is a real phenomenon behind it all.

Endnotes

1 Keel, John Mystery *Aeroplanes Of The 1930s* Part 1 FSR Volume 16 Number 3 1970 pp. 10-13
2 Quoted in the *New York Times* on 13th August 1946
3 Reported in the *Daily Telegraph* on 22nd August 1946
4 In the *Daily Telegraph* 6th September 1946
5 Fowler, Raymond *UFOs: Interplanetary Visitors* Exposition Press, New York 1974 pp.105-106
6 Quoted in the Sydney Sun 25th February 1967
7 Berlitz, Charles and Moore, William *The Roswell Incident* London 1980 pp.67-72
8 Friedman's website is found at stantonfriedman.com
9 For example, Department of the Airforce Staff Message Division, outgoing classified message, HQ USAF, AFOIN-23, 16th July 1952
10 FBI memorandum from V. P. Keay to A. H. Belmont, 29th July 1952
11 For a more comprehensive list see *Above Top Secret* by Timothy Good, Grafton Books 1989
12- The Black Aces is a Strike Fighter Squadron of VFA-41 aircraft.

13- From his interview with Joe Rogan, *The Joe Rogan Experience* #1361, 5th October 2019

Chapter Three – Military and Government Responses

Not long after the dramatic sightings over Washington DC in 1952, the Prime Minister of the United Kingdom, Winston Churchill, wrote a personal minute to the Secretary of State for Air and to Lord Cherwell asking "What does all this stuff about flying saucers amount to? What can it mean? What is the truth? Let me have a report at your convenience."(1) The response he received was intended to assure him that all sightings were no more than misidentified natural phenomena, optical illusions and delusions on the part of the witnesses.(2) Lord Cherwell even went as far as to assure the prime minister that the Americans had made significant investigations and had concluded that there was nothing of interest behind it all. In fact this was a lie, the US military had decided that the objects were real and that there were many hundred official reports supporting this conclusion, something the CIA was taking very seriously.(3)

By 1954 the Defence Minister, Earl Alexander of Tunis, wrote of the UFO phenomenon "This problem has intrigued me for a long time."(4) Lord Louis Mountbatten, Chief of the Defence Staff from 1958 to 1965, shared this fascination but reached an interesting conclusion. He had studied sightings for many years and had become convinced that rather than being craft occupied by unknown pilots, the UFOs were themselves the visitors.(5) As we shall see, Lord Mountbatten had recognised something that fits with Orthodox Christian thinking, which we shall return to shortly. He stated:

The fact that they can hover and accelerate away from the earth's gravity again and even revolve round a V2 in America (as reported by their head scientist) shows they are far ahead of us. If they really come over in a big way that may settle the capitalist-communist war. If the human race wishes to survive they may have to band together.(6)

It is interesting to note that this final remark was echoed by President Ronald Reagan in a speech he gave to the United Nations on 16th September 1983 when he said "I occasionally think how quickly our differences worldwide would vanish if we were facing an alien threat from outside this world." This was a theme the president returned to in November 1985 when he told Mikhail Gorbachev "How much easier his task and mine might be if suddenly there was a threat to this world from another species from another planet".(7) Reagan wasn't the first leader to suggest such ideas, on 1st March 1947, the the British Foreign Secretary Anthony Eden addressed a United

Nations conference with the words "Sometimes I think the people of this distracted planet will never really get together until they find someone in (sic) Mars to get mad against." The idea of using the UFO phenomenon as a means to removing national identities and boundaries is clearly a notion that has been around for a long time and is something we will consider in more depth later.

But beyond the interest of noted individuals, governments around the world have taken UFOs seriously. A few weeks after my wife's sighting, a debate took place in the House of Lords on 18th January 1979. It was instigated by the Earl of Clancarty who made the claim that someone in the government was misleading the public about UFOs and there were many of the Lords who agreed that the evidence pointed to a cover-up. One of the speakers, the Liberal spokesmen on aerospace, the Earl of Kimberley said in the debate:

UFOs have come to the fore since the end of the last World War, there are reports of them all through history. Among the papers of the late Professor Alberto Tulli, former director of the Egyptian Museum at the Vatican, was found one of the earliest known records of a fleet of flying saucers. It was written on papryus long ago in ancient Egypt—actually, it was at the time of Thutmose III, circa 1504 to 1450 BC, who, with his army witnessed the sighting of what we today would call UFOs.... this worldwide UFO invasion of every country's air space is of growing

*importance and therefore I suggest
that Parliament keeps a continuous watch on
the situation…. UFOs have been coming
in increasing numbers for 30 years since the
war, and I think it is time our people were
told the truth…. It has been reported that
the United States and the U.S.S.R. signed a
pact in 1971 to swop UFO information, but
the pact stated that they were to keep the rest
of the world in the dark. I believe that the
pact was signed so that neither super-power
would make mistakes about UFOs being
atomic missiles.*

The full debate can be read in *Hansard House of Lords Debate 18 January 1979 Volume 397 cc1246-3161246*. There was such interest in the debate that every copy of the Hansard report sold out. The Earl of Clancarty then formed the All-Party UFO Study Group which consisted of thirty peers who met each month to review cases and hear from guest speakers. The group no longer meets but on 4th March 1982 its founder once more raised the topic in the House. He demanded to know details of sightings, to which the government's spokesman, Viscount Long, said that in 1978 there were 750 sightings; in 1979 there were 550, in 1980 350 sightings, and in 1981 there were 600. He also claimed that all reports of sightings before 1967 had been destroyed. Further questions about UFOs were asked in the House of Commons on 9th March 1984, and once more the government spokesman claimed that the UFOs constituted no danger to U.K. defence. In reality the U.K. military has been investigating UFOs without public acknowledgement. Gordon Creighton, an intelligence officer of the Joint Intelligence Bureau has stated that since 1957 the Air Ministry has been conducting studies involving both RAF and CIA staff.(8) In 1965 George Langellan who served as an officer in the secret service revealed in a lecture he gave at Mourenx, Landes, that Russian and American secret services were investigating UFOs, and that despite the cold war, had collaborated on the issue. He claimed "The Flying saucers exist, their source is extra-terrestrial, and the future – relatively quite soon – should permit confirmation of this statement."(9)

One of the typical features of UFO investigations is the promise of some kind of disclosure of the truth in the near future. Certain figures have made a living promising the release of conclusive evidence for what is really happening, but the proof never comes, and as we shall see, the psychological impact of this unresolved expectation can be very negative.

In the United States the FBI continued to deny that it had any interest in UFOs right up until 1976. The denial was shown to be a lie when over a thousand pages of investigative reports were released to Dr Bruce Maccabee, a US Navy physicist, under a Freedom of Information Act request. Researchers into UFOs see this as something as a victory in their efforts to achieve full disclosure, but we must ask ourselves why, when the FBI Director Clarence Kelley had denied any interest in the topic just three years earlier(10) the documents should suddenly be made available to a member of its own military. The release of information is very carefully controlled, and later we shall consider how misinformation has played an important role in governments' response to UFOs.

In fact the U.S. government has always attempted to investigate these sightings. The once fabled but now widely documented Majestic 12 (MJ-12) group was established by President Truman in 1947 to investigate and report directly back to him.(11) It is interesting how one member of MJ-12, Dr Donald Menzel who was the Director of the Harvard College Observatory and later worked for the National Security Agency, wrote a number of books attacking the idea that UFOs were real. The MJ-12 group also included the former Director of the CIA General Hoyt Vandenberg.

In addition, high ranking officials such as Dr Lloyd Berkner who was the executive secretary of the Joint Research and Development Board, formed a special committee called the Robertson Panel at the behest of the president in 1953, to work with and report to the CIA on UFOs. Meetings were first held at the Pentagon from 14th to 17th January and for the rest of its existence only selected information was released to other officials: it only became declassified in 1975. The decision was made by the panel to undermine all sightings, regardless of who reported them. The original report from 1953 set out its aims very clearly:

The debunking aim would result in reduction in public interest in "flying saucers" which today evoke a strong psychological reaction. This education could be accompanied by mass media such as television, motion pictures and popular articles… It was felt strongly that psychologists familiar with mass psychology should advise on the nature and extent of the programme.

One of the more famous U.S. investigations was called Project Bluebook. This was a US Airforce operation that began in 1952 (following two similar investigations called Project Sign in 1947 and Project Grudge in 1950). It ran until December 1969 and took its name from the blue papers used in university examinations: it was felt that the investigation should be as thorough and detailed as a university final exam. The official response to the tens of thousands of cases that the project had investigated was released in 1968. Called the Condon Report, it judged that there was nothing of substance to the sightings, and Bluebook was officially shut down the following year. This public declaration was in sharp contrast to statements issued by Captain Edward Ruppelt who was the first Director of Project Bluebook who concluded that the objects were some kind of craft that were not produced by either the U.S. or U.S.S.R.. Project Bluebook had an officer appointed to report sightings on every US airbase and Ruppelt was given the authority to interview any officer of any rank without having to follow the usual chain of command. It was the astronomer Dr J. Allen Hynek, the scientific consultant of the project, who created the familiar categories of close encounters. He admitted that he had joined the group as a sceptic, but quickly became convinced that they were studying a real phenomenon, and he became so consumed by the subject that he devoted much of his life to continuing his research into UFOs. After Bluebook presented its findings to the Robertson Panel, the decision was made to deliberately undermine public belief in UFOs through ridicule, celebrity comments and even by enlisting the Walt Disney Company to work with psychologists. Civilian groups investigating UFOs were to be monitored because of their potential impact on public thinking. This really amounted to a decision to control public thought, what is often termed a Psy-Op (psychological operation). In 1953 it became a criminal offense for military personnel to discuss any reports on UFOs that had been judged classified with a potential two year imprisonment for disobedience.(12) Further, all Airforce staff were ordered to only discuss UFO sightings that had been found to have a conventional explanation, and any mention of unexplained sightings were forbidden.(13) In 1955 the purpose of Bluebook was changed from simply investigating UFO sightings to minimising the number of UFO reports.

In 1953 Major Donald Keyhoe Director of the National Investigations Committee on Aerial Phenomena, revealed that both the CIA and U.S. Air Force were working hard to control public thinking on UFOs. He quoted Captain Edward Ruppelt as saying:

We're ordered to hide sightings when possible, but if a strong report does get out we have to publish a fast explanation – make up something to kill the report in a hurry, and also ridicule the witness, especially if we can't figure an answer. We often have to discredit our own pilots.(14)

Despite attempts by the Airforce to smother the story, by 1960 there was sufficient public concern for U.S. Congressional hearings to be held on UFOs. Civilian research groups accused the military of a cover up, and as a result the budget for Bluebook was increased with additional staff appointed to its work. But the direction of its thinking continued to frustrate many, and criticism of how the public were being treated on the issue only grew stronger. Not least from within the project's own personnel, most notably from Hynek who went public with his feelings and listed detailed failures of the investigation: there was little official response.

But another wave of sightings in 1966(15) resulted in a Congressional Hearing by the House Committee on Armed Services at which Airforce explanations of the UFO reports were found to be false, and it was found that Airforce personnel had been confiscating newspapers from local people in order to prevent them reading about the sightings. Civilians had been told not to mention what they had seen, and the Committee acknowledged that the Airforce had deliberately attempted to ruin the reputations of police officers who had reported seeing UFOs.

A surprising detail in the U.S. government's response was to pass a law in 1954 making commercial pilots subject to military restrictions with regard to making public statements about their sightings. If pilots informed the media about seeing UFOs they could face a prison sentence of up to ten years on the grounds that such information could be vital to national security.(16)

The censorship extended to television broadcasts. On 22nd January 1958, CBS Television planned to interview Major Keyhoe. The Airforce insisted on reviewing his material and removed most of the content. They also had Air Force spokesmen undermine his evidence by presenting the silliest and most unbelievable cases so as to discredit him. Keyhoe was so unhappy with his treatment, especially at being cut off at one point as he spoke, that he published part of his intended presentation which read:

There is an official policy not to confirm the existence of UFOs until all the answers are known…In January 1955 a report by a panel of top scientists at the Pentagon reached this conclusion: There is strong circumstantial evidence, but no concrete proof that UFOs are spaceships.

These examples certainly indicate military interest in UFOs, but the true level of concern and levels of secrecy was extremely high. In the late 1950s Members of Congress were becoming uneasy. Representative William Ayres of Ohio admitted that "Congressional investigations have been held and are being held on the problem of unidentified flying objects. Since most of the material presented is classified, the hearings are never printed."(17)

The level of secrecy being imposed led Vice Admiral Roscoe Hillenkoetter, who had been the director of the CIA from 1947 to 1950, to say:
It is time for the truth to be brought out in Congressional hearings. Behind the scenes, high-Ranking Air Force officers are soberly concerned about the UFOs. But through official secrecy and ridicule, many citizens are led to believe that unknown flying objects are nonsense. To hide the facts, the Air Force has silenced its personnel through the issuance of regulation.(18)

Reports of UFOs continued to be made despite the hostile reaction that the CIA and Air Force had managed to create in the media. In 1966 the U.S. Air Force set up yet another investigation, this time through the University of Colorado. In February 1967 the group's lead scientists, Dr Edward Condon, Dr Richard Low and Dr William Price were permitted access to the CIA's National Photographic Centre to view classified images of UFOs. Despite them having Air Force backing, an internal CIA memo reveals how concerned the organisation was that the public might discover how serious they were taking UFOs:

Any work performed by the National Photographic Centre to assist Dr Condon in his Investigation will not be identified as work accomplished by the CIA. Dr Condon was advised to make no reference to the CIA in regard to this work effort.(19)

After three years of Investigation the result was a highly negative report that went to great efforts to establish its scientific neutrality while clearly doing everything it could to further undermine witnesses and their accounts.(20) Many people at the time considered it to be heavily influenced by the CIA.

Official investigations had led to great frustration amongst those making reports of sightings and it was inevitable that civilian research organisations would appear. The most influential of these was the National Investigations Committee on Aerial Phenomena (NICAP) which was founded in 1956 by Thomas Brown who had worked for the U.S. Navy as a physicist. The group included former members of the CIA as well as various ex-military personnel.(21) Despite the group's prominence in arguing for greater public disclosure of the facts about UFOs, it is interesting to note that one of its key members was Colonel Joseph Bryan III who had been the original chief of Psychological Warfare in the CIA. When this fact emerged in 1977, Keyhoe denied ever having known of Bryan's past work and Bryan himself was forced to claim he was no longer working for the CIA when he joined the group. Further suspicion is raised when we discover that the NCIAP's vice chairman, Count Nicholas de Rochefort, had also been a member of the CIA's psychological warfare staff. The point to note here is that the CIA should be so concerned about public knowledge of UFOs that it went to these lengths to infiltrate and guide the activities of the NCIAP. UFO researchers have continued to identify references in released CIA memos to UFO experts and their research, despite the CIA's insistence that it has concluded that there is nothing of importance behind the sightings.

In recent years there has been a lot of attention given to the work of the National Security Agency (NSA), not least because of Edward Snowden's revelations about its mass-surveillance of both politicians and ordinary people. The NSA was founded by President Truman in 1952. During a case of litigation by the Citizens Against UFO Secrecy (CAUS) against the CIA, the attempt was made to admit eighteen NSA documents on UFOs as evidence. The response was that the documents were exempt from disclosure under the Freedom Of Information Act. Although two documents were eventually released in 1980, suspicions about NSA interest in UFOs was confirmed that same year when the NSA representative Eugene Yeates admitted in court that there were 239 documents relating to UFOs that were being withheld. Researcher Timothy Good has made repeated attempts to obtain documents from the NSA and amongst the meagre response he has received was reference to the organisation's assessment of "Human survival implications relating to the UFO phenomena".(22) The documents reveal the NSA's perspective:

Rarely have men of science, while acting within their own professional capacities, perpetrated hoaxes. The fact that UFO phenomenon (sic.) have been witnessed all over the world from ancient times, and by considerable number of reputable scientists in recent times, indicates rather strongly that UFOs are not all hoaxes… History has shown us time and again the tragic results of a confrontation between a technologically superior civilisation and a technologically inferior people.(23)

Beyond the U.S.A. there is evidence that many countries around the world have taken the UFO phenomenon very seriously. The French government first established its investigation in 1952 and two years later the French MP Jean Nocher authorised the French Secretary for Air, M. M. Catroux, to set up a commission to distinguish between real and hoax cases. France experienced a heavy wave of sightings through 1973 and 1974, leading Robert Galley, the French Minister of Defence, to make the following statement:

A mass of reports is coming in from the airborne gendarmerie, from the mobile gendarmerie, and from the gendarmerie charged with conducting investigations. It is all pretty disturbing.(24)

Galley went on to say that a department had been set up within the French Ministry of Defence in order to deal with the many reports of UFOs. It was intended that Galley's interview would be followed with broadcasts of interviews with UFO researchers but following the broadcast with the minister, his office was burgled and the tapes were stolen (this is the official story).

Interest from the French government continued and in 1977 the Group d'Etudes Phenomienes Aerospatiaux Non Identifies (GEPAN) established a seven man committee of scientists whose task was to gather reports from the Gendarmerie. The group was given the authority by President Giscard d'Estaing to have access to laboratories across France and it worked alongside foreign agencies. There was a great deal of misinformation released about the committee, even to the point of dismissing its existence, but in 1981 Charles Hernu, the then Minister of Defence, admitted that some of GEPAN's studies had produced highly significant results.

On 6th November 1954 the Italian diplomat Dr Alberto Perego was part of huge crowds in Rome that witnessed over a hundred strange objects making "impossible" manoeuvres in the sky above them for a number of hours. Perego first enquired at the Italian Ministry of Foreign Affairs as to what was happening, but was told the government knew nothing about it. The diplomat had access to General Pezzi, Chief of the Cabinet of Air Defence, but again was told there was no official knowledge of the event.

The Spanish position has been a little more transparent since the Divisional General commanding the region around the Canary Islands, Carlos Castro Cavero, gave an interview with La Gaceta Del Norte in June 1976. General Cavero said in the interview:

As a general my opinion is the same as the air ministry, but in my own personal capacity I have for some time held the view that UFOs are extra-terrestrial craft.

He went on in the interview to say that he himself had witnessed a UFO and that the Spanish Air Ministry had at least twenty cases that had been investigated at length by scientific experts which had remained unexplainable. He confirmed that there were many countries working together to try and understand what was happening.

In Australia all reports of unidentified aircraft are dealt with by the Royal Australian Air Force. Their official term for UFOs is Unidentified Aerial Sightings (UAS) and at every base officers are appointed to respond when they are reported.(25) The Australian Air Force produces a document called Summaries of Unusual Aerial Sightings, which provides attempts to explain all sightings: it concluded that approximately three percent of all reports remain unexplained (a figure that is very similar to both U.S. and U.K. estimations). But despite this apparent low rate of incidence, the Australian government has a long history of investigating UFOs. In 1920 the ship SS Amelia J. disappeared at a time when a number of reports were being made of strange lights around the area of the Bass Straight. A rescue aeroplane was sent to recover survivors but this also vanished.(26) Reports of UFOs in this area continued to be investigated, most noticeably in 1944, and in 1952 this led the Department of Civil Aviation to establish a bureau to oversee reports of UFOs. However, members of the Australian Cabinet were concerned about the implications of these sightings and handed responsibility for the investigations into the hands of the Australian Secret Service.(27) Researcher James Holledge has revealed that these investigations were conducted with support from both the CIA and the NSA.

In 1963 Senator J. Cavanagh was denied access to an official Federal Government report on UFOs by the Minister of Air. This led to widespread public criticism, including from Dr H. Messel who was Professor of Physics at Sydney University. Accusations of a cover-up were made when the Australian government insisted that no such document existed. The arguments continued for a couple of years leading Professor Messel to say in 1965:

The facts about saucers were long tracked down and results have long been known in top secret defence circles of more countries than one. Whatever the truth, it might be regarded as inadvisable to give people at large no clue about the true nature of these things.(28)

As public interest in UFOs continued to grow, the Australian government attempted to disassociate itself with the whole subject. On 2nd May 1984 Gordon Scholes, the Defence Minister, dismissed the sightings as having no threat to national security and claimed that they were therefore of no interest.

The Canadian government has followed a similar public line, claiming little interest while maintaining a policy of misinformation. Researchers point to a memo sent from Wilbert Smith who was the senior radio engineer for the Canadian Government Department of Transport to the Controller of Telecommunications on 21st November 1953. The memo was categorised top secret and is one of the key documents used by UFO researchers to prove a government cover-up. In the memo Smith says:

The existence of a different technology is borne out by the investigations which are being carried on at the present time in relation to flying saucers.

Smith went on to claim that through his links with the Canadian Embassy in Washington, he had discovered that the U.S. government rated the level of secrecy over UFOs as being higher than that for the H-Bomb. He said that though UFOs exist, little is known or understood about them or their objectives, and that the U.S. government considered the subject to be of the highest significance. In the memo, Smith named the scientist in charge of the investigation as Dr

Vannevar Bush; the same scientist who was later discovered to have been the head of the MJ-12 group.

In response to Smith's message, in 1950 the Canadian Department of Transport set up Project Magnet. On 2nd December the Deputy Minister of Transport, Commander C. Edwards, appointed Smith as Engineer-in-Charge of the project which was tasked with the investigation of UFOs. This is a significant event because it not only reveals the government's interest, but demonstrates how seriously they took the content of Smith's memo. For Many years Canadian officials refused to acknowledge that the group existed and insisted there was no government investigation being carried out. This was revealed to be a lie when the researcher Arthur Bray obtained reports of twenty-five sightings that had been investigated by Project Magnet. The Canadian Air Force issued a number of directives through the 1950s to pilots on how they were to make reports of UFOs.

In 1968 the National Research Council took responsibility for dealing with all reports of UFOs in Canada. The year before this, on 27th May, Canadian MP Ed Schreyer attempted to raise the issue of UFOs in the House of Commons but was prevented from doing so by the Speaker Of The House. Further pressure was applied to the government, forcing Leo Cadieux, the Defence Minister, to state on 11th November 1967, "It is not the intention of the Department of National Defence to make public the reports of sightings."

It is not surprising that little information has been released from or within China about UFO sightings. But in 1978 the Chinese newspaper *The People's Daily* published an article by Slieng Heng Yen, from the Chinese Academy of Social Sciences, on the subject, and over the next two years other articles appeared in the Guang Ming Daily. Such stories represent a shift in the official Chinese perspective since nothing is permitted to be released in these publications without government approval. The stories stirred public interest and in 1980 the Chinese UFO Studies Association was established with links to Wuhan University. The association grew to have branches across China, including in Beijing, Sichuan, Shanxi, Hubei and Guangdong and was headed by Cha Leping, an astro-physicist. The group published its findings in The Journal of UFO Research which sold over 300,000 copies of its first edition. Leping was given access to hundreds of UFO sightings dating back to 1940 and he was permitted to make lengthy speaking tours to present his findings to the public.

In 1985 an article appeared in the *China Daily* which purported to set out the Official position of the Chinese Government. Entitled "UFO Conference Held in Darlian", it reported that many scientists had been given permission to meet and discuss the UFO phenomenon. Interestingly, one of the papers presented dealt with how UFOs affect the human body. The article publicised the *China UFO Research Group* which it said had over twenty-thousand members. The article concludes that UFOs are a "profound mystery"(29) that is the subject of research by governments around the world.

The situation in Russia has developed with the fall of the U.S.S.R., but the extent to which official sources have any more freedom to discuss UFOs is questionable. In 1967 Dr Felix Yarevitch Zigel was permitted to publish a story in the magazine Smena in which he declared that UFOs needed to be studied by top level scientists. Zigel was the Assistant Professor of Cosmology at the Moscow Aviation Institute, and so anything he wrote was sanctioned by the government. Zigel made reference to a history of sightings in the U.S.S.R. which he said had been investigated. The article was a turning point because prior to this only books and articles debunking UFOs had been permitted publication. In fact the CIA had learned of Soviet concerns about UFOs as early as 1952 when a double-agent named Yuri Popov had passed on documents revealing a directive that the Chief Intelligence Directorate of the Soviet General Staff were troubled by reports of UFO sightings and wanted to know of their origin and nature.(30)

Documents released under the Freedom of Information Act have revealed CIA memos that demonstrate deep concern amongst U.S. officials about whether the Soviets had a better understanding of UFOs, and whether such knowledge could be used militarily. Though this might be a concern we would expect during the

Cold War, it does demonstrate how seriously they themselves were taking the sightings. However, researcher Timothy Good has unearthed a number of documents which suggest that there was a good deal of collaboration between Soviet and U.S. scientists about UFOs even as early as the 1960s.(31)

Soviet recognition of UFO sightings became official on 18th October 1967 when the first meeting was held of the UFO section of the All-Union Committee on Cosmonauts of the DOSAAF (the Soviet Department of Defence). The committee was made up of military personnel, high ranking scientists, a cosmonaut and astronomers. The outcome of the meeting was a request to the Air Force for copies of reports of UFO sightings: the request was denied. Despite this, Dr Zigel was instructed to appear on Moscow Central Television.(32) During the broadcast, Dr Zigel instructed viewers that the UFO phenomenon was a serious issue which required detailed analysis, and he invited all Soviet citizens who had witnessed a UFO to make an official report of their sighting. Moscow newspapers reported hundreds of letters being sent to them in response to Dr Zigel's appeal, and by November 1967 General A. Getman who chaired the UFO section of the committee declared that it must be dissolved; no reason was given for the decision.

UFOs were no longer a subject the Soviet's were willing to acknowledge until 1979 when a group was established within the USSR Academy of

Sciences Institute of Terrestial Magnetism and Radioactivity to study unexplained phenomenon. Those appointed to lead this group were interviewed in *Nedelya* (*The Week*) where they went to great lengths to ridicule interest in UFOs but ended with an invitation to any witnesses to send their reports to the Academy of Sciences. This is an example of what James Oberg, a senior mission controller at NASA, believes is a use of UFO sightings as a cover story for the testing of new technology; an issue we will discuss later.

But by 1983 the Russians were acknowledging that UFOs were something beyond their explanation. On 6th January an article appeared in *Sovietskaya Kultura* describing how a UFO had flown near a Soviet Air Force jet in 1981. The article called for greater collaboration amongst scientists to solve the mystery of these sightings.(33) In February of 1984, Pavel Popovitch a former cosmonaut, was appointed head of the Commission for the Investigation of Anomalous atmospheric Phenomena in Mosow. Popovitch gave a number of interviews to various newspapers describing sightings that could not be explained and again citizens were encouraged to come forward with their reports.

Perhaps the last word from Russia should come from Mikhail Gorbachev, the former U.S.S.R. President, who in 1990 said "The phenomenon of UFOs is real and we should approach it seriously and study it."(34)

Reports of UFO sightings are very common in South America, particularly in Chile, Peru and Brazil. In the latter of these examples it is the Air Force which conducts investigations. The Air Force UFO Study Division is based in Sao Paulo, and tight control has been maintained on all UFO stories. In 1969 The Air Force issued a directive to all Brazilian government officials, even at local level, that release of information about UFOs to the press was strictly forbidden, and again in 1973 further laws were passed to limit press coverage of UFOs.(35) It may be that the UFO story provided a convenient reason for censoring any news that might reveal the Air Force's test flights.

This small selection of examples from around the world demonstrates that governments have, for a long time, been addressing the issue of UFOs. As we shall see, the release of misinformation has been a consistent feature of official response, a fact that must be kept in mind as we consider the recent release of material by the U.S. military. Therefore let us next address how the military has used the UFO phenomenon and whether the reported sightings can be understood simply as misidentification of advanced aircraft, or whether they require a different explanation.

Endnotes

1 – Churchill's minute was dated 28th July 1952

2 – Lord Cherwell wrote back on 14th August 1952

3 – A CIA memorandum sent to the Director of the CIA by H. Marshall Chadwell in September 1952 stated that since 1947 there had been over 1500 official reports.

4 – Leslie, Desmond: "Politicians And The UFO", *FSR* Vol 9 No 3, 1963 pp.8-9

5 – Ziegler, Philip; Mountbatten Collins, London 1985 p.493

6 – ibid p.494

7 – *The International Herald Tribune*, 5th December 1985

8 – Good, Timothy: *Above Top Secret – The Worldwide UFO Cover-Up* Grafton Books 1988 pp.119-120

9 – Michel, Aime: *Flying Saucers And The Straight-Line Mystery*, Criterion Books, New York 1958 pp.5-7

10 – In a letter of 25th October 1973 obtained and reproduced by Timothy Good in Above Top Secret op. cit. p.471

11 – A steady flow of documents from MJ-12 has emerged since 1984 after a top secret document from 18th November 1952 was first released by members of the secret service.

12 - Joint Army-Navy-Air Force Regulation number 146 of December 1953.

13 – In February 1953 the Air Force issued Regulation 200-2.

14 – Keyhoe, Major Donald, *Flying Saucers From Outer Space*, Henry Holy, New York 1953 p.87

15 - In 1966 there were numerous UFO reports in Massachusetts and New Hampshire.

16 – On 17th February 1954 a Joint Army-Navy Air Force Publication drawn up by the Joint-Communications-Electronics Committee.

17 – Ruppelt, Edward: *The Report On Unidentified Flying Objects*. Doubleday & Company, New York 1956 pp.41-45

18 – Analysis Of Flying Object Incidents In The U.S., Air Intelligence Report No. 100-203-79, Directorate of Intelligence and Office of National Intelligence, 10th December 1948 p.2

19 – Fawcett, Lawrence, *Clear Intent*, Prentice-Hall, New Jersey 1984 p.142

20 – Condon, Dr Edward, *Scientific Study of Unidentified Flying Objects*, Bantam, New York 1969

21 – Including Major Donald Keyhoe and Admiral Roscoe Hillenkoetter.

22 – Good, Timothy, *Above Top Secret* op. cit. p.419

23 – ibid p.420

24 – Robert Galley said this in an interview with Jean-Claude Bourret on the radio show France-Inter which was broadcast on 21st February 1974.

25 – Good, Timothy, Above Top Secret, op. cit. p.155

26 – Norman, Paul, "Countdown To Reality", *FSR* Vol. 31 No. 2 1986 p.13

27- Holledge, James, *Flying Saucers Over Australia*, Horwitz Publications, Sydney 1965 p.31

28 – Hervey, Michael, UFOs Over The Southern Hemisphere, Horwitz Publications, Sydney 1969 p.18

29 – China Daily 27th August 1985

30 – Directive UZ-11/14 of the Glavnoye Razvedyvatelnoye Upravleniye

31 – Timothy Good has reproduced some of these documents in his book *Above Top Secret*, op.cit.

32 – Zigel was broadcast on Moscow Central Television on 10th November 1967

33 – This was reported in *The Guardian* on 7th January 1984

34 – Mikhail Gorbachev made this statement in April 1990 when speaking in the Urals.

35 - In 1973 a Sao Paulo directive, Institutional Act No. 5 (State Security) informed all TV stations that they were forbidden to broadcast reports of UFOs without the Air Force approval.

Chapter Four – A Convenient Cover?

Public belief in alien space ships visiting the earth is a useful distraction for the military when one of their test flights is witnessed and reported. The intention here will be to briefly demonstrate that governments have been manipulating attitudes with disinformation, but also that the reality of the phenomenon does not completely fit with the idea that all UFOs are simply advanced aircraft. In fact what I shall try to show is that there are two different types of events taking place, and that government deception and control of the one must not lead us to lose sight of the other. Not all UFO sightings conform to the limits of a piloted craft, whether it is claimed to be terrestrial or extra-terrestrial. Witnesses frequently describe what points to non-physical phenomenon.

As we have seen, governments have made repeated claims of having no interest in UFOs for many decades, claims that have been revealed to be false. This is not something unique to the topic of UFOs; the CIA has been using movies and television to direct social attitudes and even had its own department based in Hollywood. In Russia the Komitet Gosudarstvennoi Bezopastnosti (KGB) had a disinformation unit running from 1959. Called Department D (for Dezinformatsiya) it produced fake photographs, news articles and public rumours and according to CIA estimates had a budget of more than four million dollars per year. Therefore, any leak that is sanctioned by the secret services of any country must be subjected to sceptical scrutiny. Through public denial, officials avoid having to explain exactly what they know, but through the release of inconclusive evidence they maintain enough interest amongst the populous to keep the story going. The OSS is known to have planted fake reports of sightings since 1947, some of them so outlandish that they undermine belief in UFOs, others with credible accounts from pilots and military personnel. We have also seen how the CIA has planted members of its psychological warfare group amongst civilian UFO researchers. The confusion that these conflicting stories create is typical of many psychological operations, it is also a technique used in hypnosis. When the brain is trapped in an unsolvable riddle, it becomes more vulnerable to suggestion: this is why many advertisements include strange and meaningless imagery that the rational processes of the brain try to solve. But creating this confusion also enables the secret services to control the narrative more effectively. With a clear and definite set of facts, people may accept or reject what the government is telling them, but with conflicting stories and explanations, we are left unable to discern the degree of truthfulness in government statements. One further consequence is that when enough evidence is provided to convince people something is happening, many will attempt to create theories to provide an explanation, and it further strengthens the government's hand when it is in a position to confirm or debunk a group's ideas.

The programme of misinformation is revealed in the way both the U.S. and U.K. governments have changed their claims about how they treat UFOs. For years Nick Pope appeared on U.K. television as the apparent voice of reason, debunking reports of sightings. He was a frequent guest on the less challenging morning shows, and repeatedly insisted that the government had investigated the topic and concluded that UFOs were of no interest. Pope worked for the Minsitry of Defence for twenty-one years, including from 1991 to 1994 when he had non-operational duties which included the investigation of UFO sightings; he then became a freelance journalist. In a 2009 Ministry of Defence statement listed in the government archives we are informed

The Ministry of Defence does not have any expertise or role in respect of 'UFO / flying saucer' matters or to the question of the existence or otherwise of extraterrestrial lifeforms, about which it remains totally open-minded. To date the MOD knows of no evidence which substantiates the existence of these alleged phenomena.

However, Pope was permitted to publish an article in the *New York Times* on 29th May 2019 titled "UFOs Have Come Out Of The Fringe And Into The Mainstream". In the opening paragraph he writes "After years of denial, it turns out that the U.S. government has a secret program, researching and investigating UFOs." Pope goes on to describe the Pentagon's secret programme, AATIP, and goes on to reference numerous military encounters with UFOs as well as a report sent to John McCain on January 8th 2016 of which Pope says:

The DIA disclosed that they had researched anti-gravity, warp drives, wormholes and other theoretical physics concepts needed for interstellar travel, as part of an effort to understand what they termed "foreign advanced aerospace weapon threats."

Pope made the claim that the Air Force was having to issue new guidance to its pilots in order to deal with the "upsurge in UFO activity" and he concludes that "The pace of events is picking up, and we seem to be building up to something. Something is happening. Something new. Something big." This statement was made in 2019, but of course, nothing big ever happened.

The following day on 30th May 2019 the *New York Times* followed Pope's article with an interview with Christopher Mellon, a former Deputy Assistant Secretary of Defence for Intelligence. In the article Mellon claimed that "U.S. Navy pilots who recently reported seeing

UFOs on a near-daily basis in 2014 and 2015 have legitimate concerns." He went on to say:

The pilots' concerns are, one, there have been near mid-air collisions, so there is a safety issue. Two, there is a vital national security issue which is that our sovereignty is being violated by vehicles of unknown origin.

Mellor made reference to "mystery beings" and stated that U.S. intelligence was working with NATO allies whose pilots were experiencing the same phenomenon. The idea that he would be free to make such statements without official sanction is unthinkable, and it is clear that the story was being released to serve the agenda of those controlling the information.

There is a sufficient body of evidence to demonstrate that the U.S. government particularly, is leading public interpretation to conclude that UFOs are some kind of physical craft. The tic-tac footage for example fits perfectly into the idea that we are encountering a physical means of transport, but one that is beyond our technical capabilities. While this provides a convenient way of concealing their own flight-tests, it does not explain the reports of phenomenon that include non-physical events.

From his study of UFOs, Dr Carl Jung (who was a consultant to the Aerial Phenomena Research Organisation) concluded that:

The American Air Force (despite its contradictory statements) as well as the Canadian, consider the observations to be real. However the discs do not behave in accordance with physical laws but as though without weight, and they show signs of intelligent guidance, by quasi-human pilots. What astonishes me most is that the American Air Force, despite all the information in its possession and its so-called fear of creating panic, seems to work systematically to do that very thing.(1)

We shall consider Jung in more detail in light of his occult ideas, but let us consider some examples that demonstrate this idea of UFOs being other than mechanical devices. Dr Pierre Guerin, an astrophysicist of the French Institute of Astrophysics says that those scientists who reject the reality of UFOs do so because the phenomenon does not fit into our understanding of science. He says:

Scientists are not only embarrassed by UFOs: they're furious because they don't understand them. There is no possibility of explaining them in three-dimensional space-time physics.(2)

On 29th June 1954 Captain James Howard was flying from New York to London (Flight 510-196) when he witnessed what he described as strange objects that flew alongside his passenger jet for around twenty minutes. He made drawings of the UFOs and passengers reported watching them through their windows. There was a single large object followed by half a dozen smaller ones. Captain James reported: "The large object was continually, slowly, changing shape, in the way a swarm of bees might alter its appearance."(3) He said that after a while the smaller objects merged

66

with the large one, and were tracked by ground radar.

In a U.S. Defence Intelligence Agency report of September 1976, an Iranian Air Force F-4 jet was sent to investigate bright lights being reported above Tehran. As the pilot approached the luminous object he lost control of his aircraft and all his instruments ceased working. As his jet turned away from the UFO control was returned. A second F-4 was then sent to investigate, and the pilot reported seeing a huge object with multiple lights flashing across it. An official report sent to the US Embassy stated:

Another brightly lighted object came out of the first… and then joined with the first object once more. Another object appeared to come out of the primary object going straight down, at a great rate of speed. The F-4 crew watched the object approach the ground, anticipating a large explosion. This object appeared to come gently to rest on the earth.(4)

The separating and joining of parts of a UFO is a recurrent detail and there have been accounts of many objects joining to form a single body before disappearing. The appearance and disappearance is also a characteristic that distinguishes them from mechanical craft. On 20th April 1992, on a NBC Nightly News broadcast by one of its crew in Nevada, reporter Fred Harris is heard describing the object as "something that seems to deny the laws of physics".

One of the traps many researchers into UFOs fall is to imagine that when someone with a background in the military or intelligence agencies tells them something, they feel excited to have been chosen to receive the truth. Timothy Good has fallen into this trap many times, and even Mark Pilkington, author of *Mirage Men*, who sets out to present his findings as the dispelling of UFO myths, too often relies on talkative secret service employees who he takes at face value to be insider whistle-blowers.(5) Certainly Pilkington's book demonstrates that the military has had the capacity to create fake radar signals that can give the impression that a vehicle is moving at great speed, or even appearing and disappearing, and that fake UFO events have been created by the U.S. Air Force in order to distract public attention from their other activities. He even demonstrates that for many decades, the CIA has been using UFOs as part of its psychological warfare programme, manipulating public opinion to influence the perceptions and beliefs of foreign governments about possible U.S. technology. But his findings do not explain the more bizarre experiences that many people have had, or the long history of such events extending back long before modern secret agencies have been in existence. The difficulty with many of these researchers is simply that they are looking at the issue from a purely materialistic perspective, and when they discover evidence of human deception, they assume that this must account for every kind of UFO encounter. What should become clear in the material I am presenting is that there is something happening that governments do not understand, but which they are willing to use in parallel with their own activities to reinforce the deception they are carrying out. The occult reality of what is often taking place only adds to the confusion and uncertainty surrounding the subject.

The writer Paul Dong describes how Chinese researchers have concluded that instead of UFOs travelling at great speed, they arrive by means of something called "unobservable light". This is based on the philosophy of yin and yang and proposed that unobservable light can transport objects beyond time and space in what is called camouflaged flight: camouflaged because it misleads the human senses. Chinese philosophers suggest that such movement could overcome physical barriers, such as walls and ceilings. Using the meditation methods known as chi gong, many Chinese practitioners claim not only to have experienced a psychic journey to other planets, but also encountered aliens and communicated with them.(6)

The Orthodox Christian will immediately recognise this as spiritual delusion. The non-physical nature of UFOs is often observed by non-Christians as revealing that UFOs have a "spiritual" nature. This is a belief that has become more common as new age ideas have been accepted into mainstream western culture. There are also a number of official voices supporting this idea, and the link between occult practices and UFOs is growing stronger; interest in UFOs is often a gateway to exploration of occultism. We must be clear that many Church Fathers have made a distinction between what is perceived as "spiritual" and what is good. Before looking in detail at what the Orthodox Church teaches us about the true nature of the UFO phenomenon, let us identify how different interpretations are guiding enquirers towards the occult.

Endnotes

1 – Jung, Carl, "On Unidentified Flying Objects", *FSR* Vol. 1 no 2 1955 p.18

2 – Good, Timothy, *Above Top Secret* op.cit. p.133

3 – Howard, James, "The BOAC Labrador Sighting of 1954" *FSR* Vol. 27 No. 6 1981 p.3

4 – Report sent by the Defence Atache, U.S. Embassy, Tehran to the DIA and released to researcher Charles Huffer in 1977.

5 – Pilkington, Mark, *Mirage Men, A Journey In Disinformation, Paranoia and UFOs,* Constable, London, 2010

6 – Dong, Paul "The Yin and Yang of UFOs", *Alien Update*, Random House, Auckland 1993 p.73

Chapter Five – SETI

The belief that UFOs are an indication of extra-terrestrial life has resulted in the multi-million dollar project known as SETI (search for extra-terrestrial intelligence), though today most of its budget comes from private donations. The programme originates with John D. Kraus who argued in an article in the March 1955 issue of Scientific American that the cosmos should be scanned for radio signals, since he believed that this was the most likely way contact would be made. Less than two years later, Ohio University was given a grant of seventy-one thousand dollars to build a radio telescope to carry out the task. The money came from the National Science Foundation: in 1950s America this was a huge sum of money. The telescope was built over an area of twenty acres and was nicknamed "Big Ear".

In fact the idea for this kind of search goes back much further. In 1896, Nikola Tesla attempted to contact the inhabitants of Mars using his wireless electrical transmission system. Three years later he even believed he had detected a repetitive signal that indicated alien life, but which contemporary scientists believe was coming from Europe or was the natural signals generated around the earth.

The orbit of the planets brings them closer at certain times, and on 21st August 1924 the whole of the U.S.A. was encouraged to enter three days of periodic radio silence in order for researchers to listen out for signals that might be coming from Mars, which was close to earth at that time. It was called "National Radio Silence Day" and for five minutes on every hour, broadcasts were cut off. A receiver was sent by balloon nearly two miles into the air to make contact, but no one was calling.

Other attempts continued to be made, including in 1960 the use of a telescope twenty-six metres in diameter at Green Bank, West Virginia. In the same decade the Soviets, led by the astronomer Iosif Shklovsky, positioned multiple antennas across the U.S.S.R. to detect signals, but again the search was fruitless. Shklovsky went on to write the influential book Universe, Life, Intelligence in 1962, which had a great influence on the thinking of Carl Sagan, who we shall consider in detail later.

In 1971 NASA took an interest and a report was produced which recommended spending ten billion dollars on a massive collection of dishes called Project Cyclops. Though the budget was deemed too high, the result was an increased interest in SETI and in 1980, Carl Sagan, Bruce Murray, and Louis Friedman founded the U.S. Planetary Society, which had as a major aim, the continuation and expansion of SETI studies. It is interesting to note that later funding also came in part from

Steven Spielberg, who wrote and directed the movie *Close Encounters of The Third Kind* (1977) and directed *E.T.* (1982).

There was a good deal of criticism about the amount of money being spent on the SETI programme, chief critic was Senator William Proxmire, and Congress removed its funding from the NASA budget in 1981. But in 1982 the funding was restored after an intense publicity campaign by Carl Sagan, and ten years later the U.S. government began a long-term SETI programme, scanning large portions of the sky using a forty three metre radio telescope of the National Radio Astronomy Observatory as well as an observatory in Puerto Rico. The programme was ridiculed by a number of members of Congress, but was able to continue when private investors backed the project. In 2012 Franklin Antonio, Co-Founder and Chief Scientist of QUALCOMM Incorporated invested three and a half million dollars into the programme, but this was small change compared with the hundred million dollars committed in 2015 to maintain what was called Breakthrough Listen, based at Berkeley SETI Research Centre, located in the Astronomy Department at the University of California, Berkeley. Today, the SETI Institute uses a specially designed instrument for its SETI efforts, the Allen Telescope Array (ATA) located in the Cascade Mountains of California which, it is claimed, can monitor the entire night sky simultaneously.

The U.S.A. is not alone in searching for alien transmissions. In China the National Development and Reform Commission has funded the use of a five hundred metre Aperture Spherical Telescope. This is notable because it is the world's first observatory built with SETI as its primary objective.

Computers all around the world are now participating in the SETI programme. Using a downloadable piece of software, anyone can allow the seti@home project to use their idle computer power, and so far nearly three hundred thousand computers have been used this way. After ten years this has allowed the SETI programme to listen to approximately twenty per cent of the sky. This has developed into SETI.Net which is equipment that anyone can buy that uses an antenna at home to contribute to the search. The programme now includes search for laser and gamma ray signals and for technosignatures, which is the search for signs of industrial or technological processes such as persistent light signals or artificially created radiation.

SETI scientists have created the term astrobiology. On their website, the SETI Institute describes astrobiology as a search for extraterrestrial life using the disciplines of astronomy, geology, biology, and sociology. It has at its foundation the *Drake Equation*, a means they say of calculating how many technologically advanced civilisations there must be in our galaxy. It takes its name from the astronomer Frank Drake who in the 1950s wanted to establish how and where we should look for alien life. In particular,

Drake focussed on what kinds of planets would be suitable for the development of life, and this has been expanded to examine asteroids and meteors and how they might be the means for the biological ingredients to be carried from one part of the galaxy to another to spread life. Drake developed his equation in 1961 as a way of calculating how many advanced civilisations we should expect there to be in our galaxy which we could communicate with. Carl Sagan was very impressed with Drake's work and declared that we should expect there to be at least a million alien civilisations in our Milky Way, which would only require there to be one in every hundred thousand star systems: not unreasonable one might suppose, but as we shall see, even from within his own paradigm, new scientific discoveries have made this highly unlikely. But even as SETI supporter Bernard Oliver observed, the Drake Equation is really "a way of compressing a large amount of ignorance into small space."(1)

Despite this ongoing attempt to identify extra-terrestrial transmissions, nothing has been found. This has forced those who believe in life on other planets to admit that this is strange if other civilisations are really out there; those involved in SETI call it "the great silence". The fact is, as the Italian physicist Enrico Fermi said in the 1950s, if technologically advanced civilizations are common in the universe, we should be able to detect them. In the face of cosmic silence, he coined the phrase "where is everybody?" Over time this became known as the Fermi Paradox, which simply states that if we believe the universe is as old as science claims, and that life is a random process that can occur on any suitable planet, then this is logically inconsistent with our lack of observational evidence. The physicist and Noble laureate Enrico Fermi (1901 – 1954) famously turned to his fellow scientists at Alamos in New Mexico and said "If there are extra-terrestrials, where are they?"(2) But here we see scientists determined to ignore the evidence and persist with their belief that life is the result of chemical reactions that can produce intelligent creatures if evolution is given enough time: this philosophy will be considered in detail in a later chapter. Devotees of SETI explain the failure in terms of their own flawed approach, and insist that with an improved methodology they will find the evidence that supports their theory. One might ask whether the so-called scientific method should suggest accepting the evidence and changing their hypothesis, but such is the desire to prove their theory of how life begins, they commit themselves to further decades of searching. Despite the amount of money coming from universities and governments, SETI should not be called scientific because there is no clear point at which negative results can cause the hypothesis of extraterrestrial intelligence to be abandoned. Meanwhile NASA continues to release items for news broadcasts telling us of yet more earth-like planets that are being found, maintaining the sense that we are forever on the verge of finding our cosmic neighbours. In fact, even amongst NASA scientists, there is a growing realisation that our planet is not the ordinary and common place SETI enthusiasts would have us believe, in fact, quite the opposite. But before we consider this, let us pause to reflect on one of SETI's most famous supporters, Carl Sagan.

Endnotes

1 - Dick, Steven, *Life On Other Worlds*, Cambridge University Press, Cambrige 1966 p.285
2 – ibid. Dick p.218

Chapter Six – Carl Sagan And The Unexceptional Earth

Within the SETI institute is the *Carl Sagan Centre for Research*, where over eighty scientists have as their stated goal, the explanation of how life develops. It is crucial to recognise that this has both philosophical implications and motivations: it is not simply a set of scientists working to discover the secrets that sit within nature just waiting to be found, but a group with the specific aim of proving its philosophical and theological beliefs.

Carl Sagan (1934-1996) has been a major figure in promoting the idea that there must be life beyond Earth. He was the astrophysicist who decided what would be on the discs sent out into space on the Voyager space craft in 1977, described as an introduction of ourselves to which ever alien species happened to find it.(1)

An associate professor at both Harvard and Cornell, his influence cannot be over-estimated. He wrote the most widely watched television series on American public television at that time (1980), Cosmos, as well as a number of popular science texts and novels.(2) Though he found popularity amongst the public, there were many academics who criticised him. Keay Davidson accused him of being "non-rigorous, and self-aggrandizing"(3) while Nobel Prize winning chemist Harold Urey (1893 – 1981) rejected Sagan's undisciplined and casual approach to science.(4) Urey's opinion of Sagan's work was the basis for the latter being denied tenure at Harvard. A further issue with Sagan's thinking was his belief that the "Great Silence" of the Fermi Paradox could be explained by the limited lifespan of developed species: he concluded that once a species becomes technologically advanced it will inevitably make itself extinct. This led him to become an advocate of various social issues, such as ecology and nuclear power.

Though these kinds of criticisms of Carl Sagan are legitimate, for the Orthodox Christian there is much more to be concerned about in his theories and work. Sagan was driven by an obsessive atheism that coloured everything he wrote. It is this atheism that insists that life must exist elsewhere on other planets because it cannot permit the possibility that the Earth and life here is in anyway unique. As we shall see, this led him to exaggerate the Copernicus Principle.

In the book version of his television series, *Cosmos*, he sets out his philosophy immediately; on the second page of the first chapter he states "The cosmos is all that is or ever was or ever will be."(5) In a kind of parody of the opening of the Gospel according to Saint John, Sagan establishes his belief that it is the physical universe itself that was in the beginning, not the Holy Trinity. He goes on to throw in casual statements without any scientific or philosophical argument, such as "Every star may be a sun to someone"(6) which, as we shall see, is wholly confused about what is required for the Earth to sustain life. His defence for such statements comes in the form of hopeful musings, he says "Why should we, tucked away in some forgotten corner of the cosmos, be so fortunate?"(7) Who it is that might be doing the forgetting he doesn't explain. Sagan's atheism morphs into pantheism just a couple of pages later when he states "The Earth is our home, our parent."(8)

Sagan is open with his readers (and TV viewers) when he acknowledges the true motive for his longing to prove alien life exists. He says

The nature of life on earth and the search for life elsewhere are two sides of the same question - the search for who we are.(9)

He was so sure of his beliefs that he describes the discovery of extra-terrestrials as being a "cosmic inevitability". It is with this sense of inevitability that he proceeds to tell his audience that life will be found, that we are nothing special, and that we exist as a result of random chemical reactions which through a process of impersonal selection results in us. God has no place in this process because once the proof is found it will be shown that religion is the thinking of ignorance. He says "All life on Earth is closely related. We have a common organic chemistry and a common evolutionary heritage."(10) How can Sagan be so sure? He tells us on page 40: "Evolution is a fact, not a theory." Sagan reveals his own emotional and psychological desire to deny God when he says:

A Designer is natural, appealing, and an altogether human explanation of the biological world. But, as Darwin and Wallace showed, there is another way, equally appealing, equally human, and far more compelling: natural selection, which makes the music of life more beautiful as the aeons pass.(11)

Even Darwin acknowledged in *The Origin of Species* that the Cambrian Explosion is geological evidence that is in conflict with the theory of a common ancestor. In a relatively short geological period, many kinds of life came into existence without any fossil connection with the life forms that existed before them. Sagan at least mentions this but says "Soon after the Cambrian Explosion the oceans teemed with many different forms of life" but offers no explanation of how they got there.(12) Darwin stated that once the fossil records were explored more fully, the evidence to support evolution would be found. With similar motives to Sagan's search for E.T.s, geologists have dug and scraped every corner of the earth, only to discover that the Cambrian Explosion occurred over an even shorter period than Darwin had imagined (or feared). Sagan brushes this off with the claim that the soft-tissued creatures that lived before the Cambrian Explosion would have left no fossil, but this has been proven to be false, and many fossils of soft tissues pre-existing the Explosion have been found, but none of them demonstrating any evolutionary link with the life that suddenly appeared.

Sagan's confused philosophy takes a different turn when he uses the language of Plato's forms to suggest the eternal nature of geometry. He quotes Kepler as saying:

Geometry existed before the Creation. It is co-eternal with the mind of God…
Geometry provided God with a model for the creation…Geometry is God Himself.(13)

Sagan manages to simultaneously believe two entirely opposed ideas about the Earth. He dismisses its value or uniqueness when comparing it to some of the bigger planets when he says: "These are serious planets, not fragmentary worldlets like the Earth",(14) but then attempts to present himself as a concerned ecologist when he worries about the effect of cutting down forests for farming:

Forests are darker than grasslands, and grasslands are darker than deserts. As a consequence, the amount of sunlight that is absorbed by the ground has been declining, and by changes in the land use we are lowering the surface temperature of our planet. Might this cooling increase the size of the solar ice cap, which, because it is bright, will reflect still more sunlight from the Earth, further cooling the planet, driving a runaway albedo effect?(15)

It is interesting to note that *Cosmos* was first published in 1981 and the T.V. series aired in 1980, and Sagan's primary concern about man's activities impacting the climate are that it could reduce temperature; clearly the United Nations had not yet started to issue its global warming script to the media.

Sagan's dismissal of the special nature of the Earth extends to the creatures living on it, particularly human beings. Though he places a high value on intelligence, particularly the highly developed kind that can produce vehicles to travel to other planets, he does not consider the existence of human life as being anything extraordinary. Since the random collision of chemicals in the primordial "soup" can produce life, why should whatever it happens to evolve into be of particular value? He even suggests that biologists might one day master the art of creating human life, although he humbly acknowledges that this "is far beyond our capability and will probably be so for a very long time."(16) Note again the implied inevitability of this expectation. So inevitable is this creation that he manages to see it everywhere, he says "the colours of Jupiter speak to us of chemical events that, four billion years ago back on Earth, led to the origins of life."(17) As we shall see, Sagan's assumptions were based on the limited scientific knowledge of his day which has since grown to a point where his beliefs have found to be false.

Alongside his questionable understanding of the environment, Sagan quotes the mistaken idea that human development in the womb mirrors and demonstrates the slow process of evolution. He says "In our individual embryonic development we retrace the evolutionary history of the species."(18)

Sagan is not so much making errors as using popular myths and scientific misconceptions to prove his points. His philosophy is not just atheistic, it is anti-faith and anti-God. Talking about the Pythagoreans he reveals too much of his bias when he says "like all orthodox religions, they practiced a rigidity that prevented them from correcting their errors."(19) As is always the case for those who reject God, he holds a particular grudge against Christianity, creating and dismissing a straw man when he writes "The Platonists and their Christian successors held the peculiar notion that the Earth was tainted and somehow nasty, while the heavens were perfect and divine."(20) An odd comment from a man who considers the earth nothing more than a forgettable little speck while Christians maintain that the whole Earth is an icon of God. Sagan continues:

Where are we? Who are we? We find that we live on an insignificant planet of a humdrum star lost between two spiral arms in the outskirts of a galaxy…tucked away in some forgotten corner of a universe…if we are to deal with the Cosmos, we must first understand it, even if our hopes for some unearned preferential status are, in the process, contravened.(21)

Sagan's thinking is clearly influenced by his realisation of the size of the universe. Rather than

84

recognising that its immense, unimaginable size points to the majesty of God and the limits of man, he concluded that it must mean our existence is insignificant. But understanding the physical distance between stars, it did at least bring him to the conclusion that physical travel between planets is not possible. Sagan rejected the idea that UFOs could be extra-terrestrial visitors, which is partly why he was such a keen supporter of SETI, since he believed it would be the only way to prove his theories about the origin of life. He writes:

The two Voyager interstellar spacecraft, the fastest machines ever launched from Earth, are now travelling at one ten-thousandth the speed of light. They would need forty thousand years to go to the nearest star. Do we have any hope of leaving Earth and traversing the immense distances? (22)

In Chapter Nine of *Cosmos* Sagan goes beyond a suggestion of pantheism to invoke Egyptian gods as a part of our existence. He begins the chapter with a direct quotation which he calls "an incantation from Ptolemaic Egypt" that talks about Ra the sun god separating night from day.(23) Later in the chapter he adds his own perspective on the Sun's role in our coming into being:

When the Sun turned on, its ultraviolet radiation poured into the atmosphere of the Earth; its warmth generated lightning; and these energy sources sparked the complex organic molecules that led to the origin of life.(24)

85

But suggestion is not enough, and Sagan concludes:

Our ancestors worshiped the Sun, and they were far from foolish…if we must worship a power greater than ourselves, does it not make sense to revere the Sun and stars?(25)

This statement not only questions why we should worship God as being greater than us, but seeks to claim the reasonableness and logic of worshiping the Sun if we really must satisfy these primitive needs. Sagan then introduces Chapter Ten with a quotation from a ninth century Indian legend which says:

Some foolish men declare that a Creator made The world. The doctrine that the world was created is ill-advised, and should be rejected.(26)

In Sagan's thinking we see the consequence of this rejection of God and the belief in evolution; the reduction of man to an ultimately purposeless entity. His most disturbing expression of this comes when he concludes that in order for a technological civilisation to advance, it must reduce the number of its members. He writes:

No civilisation can possibly survive to an interstellar spacefaring phase unless it limits numbers. Any society with a marked population explosion will be forced to devote all its energies and technological skills to feeding and caring for the population on its home planet. This is a very powerful conclusion and is in no way based on the idiosyncrasies of a particular civilisation… any civilisation that engages in serious

*interstellar exploration and colonisation must
have exercised zero population growth or
something very close to it for many
generations.*(27)

However powerful Sagan finds the argument for
population control to achieve the ultimate goal of
leaving the Earth, like all those who propose such
theories, he did not consider the programme should
start with him: he had five children from his three
marriages. In keeping with many such thinkers, he
promotes the United Nations' doctrines of the
destruction of national and cultural identities, and
sees the cosmic understanding of our existence to
mean that all such concepts are primitive and
dangerous. He argues:

*National boundaries are not evident when we
view the Earth from space. Fanatical ethnic or
religious or national chauvinisms are a little
difficult to maintain when we see our planet as a
fragile blue crescent fading to become an
inconspicuous point of light.*(28)

Sagan does not identify which aspects of
religious and ethnic identity he considers fanatical
or chauvinistic, and it is clear that he considers
clinging to any of these out-dated ideologies to be a
barrier to the kind of progress he envisions. The
rapid shift to globalism that has stripped nations of
cultural, political and religious diversity has rested
on exactly these kinds of philosophies, under the
banner of our common humanity; the coming one
world religion of antichrist will require widespread
acceptance of these lies.

87

Throughout Cosmos Sagan quotes texts from various myths and legends from a variety of cultures and religions; but never Christianity. He throws in teachings from the Tao Te Ching(29), from Hinduism(30), the teachings of the Buddha(31) and even Zoroastrian texts(32), and creates the illusion of being open-minded and appropriately pluralistic. But in reality he sees any traditional faith which tries to defend its doctrines as something to be overcome. Again he states:

Should we not then be willing to explore vigorously, in every nation, major changes in the traditional way of doing things, a fundamental redesign of economic, political, social and religious institutions?(33)

Words now echoed by various elite groups such as the World Economic Forum, in their push for what they call *The Great Reset*. Separating people from the institution and teachings of the Church has been a satanic goal since Pentecost, and the latest form of attack comes through the fake promises of technology. It is worth noting too that here we see the consequence of evolutionary theory. It has two demonic ideas, the first that man is the product of impersonal biological processes, but also that in the future he will be so much more advanced in every way, including morally. While the old man is portrayed as seeing himself as made in God's image and sharing a national identity with the people of his country, the evolved man of the future will have broken free of these restraints to create new and improved ways of living. Sagan does not leave us guessing at what this new morality will look like, he reveals that it will be a life of promiscuity and an absence of self-restraint that he imagines will rid us of our innate violent tendencies. Drawing on the teachings of the neuropyscologist James Prescott, Sagan claims:

Cultures with a predisposition for violence are composed of individuals who have been deprived – during at least one of two critical stages in life, infancy and adolescence – of the pleasures of the body...where infants are physically punished, there tends to be slavery, frequent killing, torturing and mutilation of enemies, a devotion to the inferiority of women, and a belief in one or more supernatural beings who intervene in our daily life.(34)

By this point Sagan has decided that faith in God is as much a hangover from our unevolved past as is mutilating people and the keeping of slaves. But he offers an answer. If our ultimate goal is technological advancement, then the new religion must be science. Sagan declares that it will replace "the fleeting comforts of superstition"(35) because for science "there are no sacred truths",(36) and so it will release us from "the abject surrender to mysticism".(37)

Ultimately, Sagan's cosmology leads him to see man's worth as being an expression of the value of the cosmos itself. In praise of the universe he writes:

The ash of stellar alchemy was now emerging into consciousness. At an ever-increasing pace,

*it invented writing, cities, art and science, and
sent spaceships to the planets and stars. These
are some of the things that hydrogen atoms can
do, given fifteen billion years of cosmic
evolution.*(38)

Sagan's rejection of the Earth as having any
unique value was based on his extension and
misappropriation of something called *The
Copernican Principle*.(39) It is this that has been the
philosophical basis for assumptions about life on
Earth and the rest of the universe, and as we shall
see, the attempt to use it as a means of proving
Earth's mediocrity has been radically challenged
by contemporary scientific discoveries about what
is necessary for life to exist on Earth.

In 1990 Voyager 1 had reached a distance of four
billion miles from the Earth. The technicians
controlling it manoeuvred it in order to look back
and photograph the Earth. The resulting image is
dramatic. Our planet appears as a stunning blue
sphere sitting in the surrounding darkness. At that
moment a shaft of light from the Sun fell directly
on us, only adding to the sense of awe and mystery
that the image can suggest. But Sagan looks with a
very different set of eyes. In his book Pale Blue
Dot he chooses to characterise what we see in the
photograph according to his own beliefs, he writes:

*Because of the reflection of sunlight...Earth
seems to be sitting in a beam of light, as if there
were some significance to this small world. But
it's just an accident of geometry and optics...Our
posturings, our imagined self-importance, the*

delusion that we have some privileged position in the Universe are challenged by this point of pale of light. Our planet is a lonely speck in the great enveloping cosmic dark. In our obscurity, in all this vastness, there is no hint that help will come to save us.(40)

In fact it is Sagan's atheism that creates an emptiness, one that he endures within himself rather than being a fact of the external universe. In the 1997 movie *Contact*, written by Sagan, the main character encounters an alien being and questions him about the purpose of communication between various alien races. The wise alien tells her that "In all our searching, the only thing that makes the emptiness bearable is each other." Here Sagan is acknowledging the reason for his yearning for ETs to exist, because without them he imagines human life is alone and purposeless. This is not just Sagan's view, but a shared philosophy amongst those working for SETI. In 2001, Seth Shostak gave a lecture on behalf of the SETI Institute as part of the Templeton Foundation lectures which had as their title *The Search For Extraterrestrials And The end of Traditional Religion*. As part of his lecture Shostak claimed that the discovery of intelligent ETs would destroy traditional religious belief on Earth. Other researchers have tried to suggest that in order to survive, religions must incorporate the existence of ETs into their teaching. As we shall see, the Vatican is certainly trying to do this, but this is not what SETI enthusiasts really mean. The astronomer Steven Dick argues that to do so religions must adopt entirely new "cosmotheological principles" which turn out to be equating God with the universe itself.

Endnotes

1 – The two "Voyager Golden Records" contain a variety of images and sounds that Sagan believed reflected human life though even if Sagan was right, it will be forty thousand years before Voyager 1 passes within 1.6 light-years' distance of the star Gliese 445 in the constellation Camelopardalis. By today's digital standards, the one hundred and fifteen images contained on the discs are a very limited snap shot of human existence.

2 – Sagan's works include *The Dragons of Eden, Pale Blue Dot, Cosmos,* and *Broca's Brain.*

3 - Davidson, Keay (1999). *Carl Sagan: A Life*. New York: John Wiley & Sons p. 227

4 – ibid. Davidson p.203

5 – Sagan, Carl, *Cosmos*, Abacus, London 2017 p.20

6 – ibid. Sagan p.20

7 – ibid. Sagan p. 22

8 – ibid. Sagan p. 24

9 – ibid. Sagan p. 35

10 – ibid. Sagan p. 36

11 – ibid. Sagan p. 42

12 – ibid. Sagan p. 47

13 – ibid. Sagan p. 70

14 – ibid. Sagan p. 104

15 – ibid. Sagan p. 122

16 – ibid. Sagan p. 150

17 – ibid. Sagan p. 175

18 – ibid. Sagan p. 188

19 – ibid. Sagan p. 208

20 – ibid. Sagan p. 213

21 – ibid. Sagan pp. 218 – 219

22 – ibid. Sagan pp. 224 – 225

23 – ibid. Sagan p. 241

24 – ibid. Sagan p. 256

25 – ibid. Sagan p. 266

26 – ibid. Sagan p. 268

27 – ibid. Sagan pp. 340 – 341

28 – ibid. Sagam p.348

29 – ibid. Sagan p. 268

30 – ibid. Sagan p. 269

31 – ibid. Sagan p. 92

32 – ibid. Sagan p. 58

34 – ibid. Sagan p. 360

35 – ibid. Sagan p. 362

36 – ibid. Sagan p. 362

37 – ibid. Sagan p. 365
38 – ibid. Sagan p. 370
39 – Sagan, Carl, *Pale Blue Dot*, Ballantine Books, New York 1994 p.7
40 – Dick, Steven, *"Cosmotheology: Theological Implications On The New Universe", Many Worlds* Dibner Library Lectures, Smithsonian Institution Series, Washington DC 2000 pp. 14-25

Chapter Seven – Life On Earth

Nicolaus Copernicus (1473 – 1543) was a Polish mathematician and astronomer who recognised that the Earth orbits the Sun, rather than the Earth being at the centre of the universe (the Ptolemaic system). As is often the case in science, this had been understood eighteen centuries earlier by Aristarchus of Samos, but from his writings it is believed that Copernicus reached this conclusion from his own observations. In the year that he died he published his major work *De Revolutionibus Orbium Coelestium* (*On the Revolutions of the Celestial Spheres*) which resulted in what became known as the "Copernican Revolution". Contrary to the popular myth, Copernicus was not persecuted and actually died of a natural cause. It is difficult for modern thinkers to grasp just how dramatic Copernicus' discoveries really were. Prior to this the accepted understanding of the universe was based on the Aristotelian model which placed the Earth at the centre of the solar system. This was seen as giving the Earth a special significance since not only did the heavens move around the Earth, but humanity was given a unique view of the cosmos (as we shall see, even NASA scientists have recognised that there is more to this principle than may be immediately apparent). Sagan combined this idea with the discovery in 1924 by Edwin Hubble (1889–1953) that our galaxy, the Milky Way, is not the entirety of the universe, but that there exist many billions of galaxies.

The Copernican Principle(1) came to mean that there were no special observers from any particular place, something which seemed to challenge a literal interpretation of the Genesis account of Creation. Those who rejected God were quick to insist that this new way of understanding man's place in the cosmos meant all moral and religious assumptions should be challenged. Philosophers proposed an entirely new way of seeing man, one that stripped him of any special role or purpose. Stephen Hawking in *The Grand Design* developed the principle to argue that it is a convincing scientific demonstration that the existence of the universe has no relationship to the existence of man, and that our appearance within it is of no cosmic significance.

Contemporary science has moved on from this interpretation of The Copernican Principle, and the anthropic principle has been used to challenge the notion that man is of no particular cosmic significance. Starting with the recognition that simply by existing at all, human life demonstrates that the forces and values of these forces within which the universe operates are consistent with our existence. Others have questioned whether we can suggest that these forces could be anything other than they are; ultimately the question becomes one of whether we choose to interpret their values as a random coincidence that happens to favour us, or whether the complexity and necessity of so many aspects of the universe being the way they are in order for man to exist demonstrates a Creator. The principle here is a familiar one in philosophy; if we were to find a watch in the forest, could we assume that its complexity and design suggest anything but an intelligent mind behind its existence? This was the question first raised by William Paley in his book *Natural Theology*, a text that Charles Darwin attempted to refute by arguing that natural selection and random variations could mimic the work of a creator or designer. Writers such as Dennis Danielson have also argued that Sagan and others have simply taken empirical evidence without making sufficient links or providing logical steps, and have not only implied a conclusion but claimed the observations are proof of metaphysical realities. Sagan was really continuing the false assumptions of Harlow Shapley who coined the phrase *The Copernican Principle* in the Nineteenth Century, and despite advances in scientific discovery to challenge it, Sagan managed to insert it into popular thinking.

We should note that in the last few decades there has been a resurgence in the theory that the Earth occupies a central place in the cosmos. Amongst others, the Roman Catholic philosopher Robert Sungenis, has argued for what has become known as the "geocentric theory" which states that the entire universe moves around the Earth. Though not geocentric, Einstein's Theory of Relativity states that the Sun, the Earth, the Moon, Jupiter, or any other point, could be chosen as a centre of the Solar System with equal validity. Sadly the Roman Catholic persecution of Galileo (1564 –1642) has tainted the perception of any theory that dares promote the beliefs of his tormentors, and those who cling to The Copernican Principle as a denial of God frequently make reference to the injustice of his treatment as proof that anyone who considers the Earth to have a special significance is an echo of Vatican brutality: a good deal of Sagan's Cosmos series was devoted to scientific martyrs in the hands of religious savages. What he fails to mention is that Galileo was arrested because the other "scientific" scholars at his university refused the revelations of his telescope and that despite popular misconception, he actually continued to receive a pension from the Roman Catholic Church until he died.

The theological question here is whether we can interpret biblical teachings according to observation. This is supposedly the very foundation of the scientific method (unless you work for SETI), and forms the basis of many people's own personal understanding of the world around them. There are two difficulties here: there were countless witnesses, many of whom gave their lives rather than deny what they had seen, who testified to the miracles of Jesus and to His death and resurrection.   Through human history the vast majority of people who have ever lived have been religious in some way, and even today one third of people living on Earth have a faith in Christ. The sheer weight of human experience is a significant piece of evidence, but science refutes it because it is not an experience that atheists can reproduce for themselves in the laboratory. The second difficulty is quite the opposite. We cannot reduce revealed truth to the status of the kinds of knowledge that is verifiable through human rational thinking. We cannot reduce any spiritual event to what is observable. Until Hubble's discovery in 1924, scientific observation led to the teaching that our galaxy is the entire universe. Any philosophical or theological assumptions based on such observations will always be changing, but revealed truth cannot be interpreted by the limited scientific findings of the day.

A good example of this is the issue of Dark Matter and Dark Energy. In the 1930s, the Swiss astronomer Fritz Zwicky observed that according to their mass, distant galaxies were orbiting one another much quicker than they should, and his conclusion was that an invisible substance exists that exerts additional gravity on objects in space. Contemporary scientists have theorised that this mysterious substance is six times more abundant than anything we can see. This is important because while accepting its existence, contemporary science cannot say where exactly it is to be found or what it is; whether it consists of one or more particles; what kinds of forces act on it; whether gravity is the only force through which it acts on other objects; how it is spread through the universe and why it should be more dense in some places than others; whether dark matter has any electrical charge, and if dark matter even really exists.(2) Similarly, astronomers are now basing their hypothesis on the idea that there is also something called dark energy which is equally mysterious.

With such changing evidence, science is not the basis on which we can establish eternal truths. The paradigms shift and beliefs that have apparently been confirmed by observation are overthrown and replaced with new ones.(3) Those who cling to the scientific model maintain that this is exactly the procedure that makes scientific discovery reliable, because it fits its understanding of the world to the latest evidence. However, since scientific understanding not only changes, but even rejects ideas that have gone before, for man experiencing a limited timespan during whatever theories are fashionable in his age, the gamble of risking his eternal salvation on such shifting sands demands a very strong faith in the science of his day.

However, the idea that science and religion are inevitably opposed in their conclusions is false. There are many high level astronomers, physicists and leaders in other scientific fields that recognise their work as pointing to a confirmation of Christian belief. In his book *Lucky Planet*, David Waltham writes that:

Earth was blessed with incredible good fortune,

100

giving it all the right properties to sustain a
complex and beautiful biosphere. It may just be
the luckiest planet in the visible Universe.(4)

In fact the Earth's capacity to sustain life relies on many factors. The mainstream media frequently celebrates NASA's discovery of new exoplanets (planets orbiting stars other than our Sun) as fresh evidence for the inevitability of the discovery of life beyond Earth. But for NASA scientists, the existence of a planet is far from proof of the likelihood of life, we only have to look at our own solar system to see how inhospitable other planets can be. The first and most important detail that NASA scientists believe will indicate the possibility of life is liquid water.

The Earth's surface is seventy percent water, at places reaching a depth of eleven thousand metres. Water is considered essential for life because of its many different qualities. For example, liquid water is a universal solvent which enables nutrients essential for life to be carried around the world, making it also an ideal medium for chemical reactions. Water not only transports different molecules to places where reactions may occur, but does so while maintaining their integrity. Its very transparency is something we might take for granted, but without it light could not penetrate to the organisms within the ocean depths, and sea creatures would be blind. Water expands when it freezes (which is why our pipes get split in winter) but this expansion reduces its density and so it floats. This results in ice floating to the surface of the oceans, rather than the body of water freezing and killing anything living within it. This also acts to insulate the body of water and so prevent further loss of heat. If ice were denser than liquid water it would sink to the bottom of the ocean and never melt. Ice at the surface is important in helping to regulate our planet's capacity to absorb or reflect sunlight, which regulates the global climate. Water absorbs heat and circulates it around the Earth, acting as a giant thermostat that regulates the temperature of our seasons. Without this we would experience extremes of temperature that make life difficult, if not impossible.

But the presence of liquid water is far from being the only factor necessary for life. There is a relatively thin band within which a planet must orbit its star if life is to exist. If the planet is either side of this band, then it will be too close or too far away. It is affectionately known as the "Goldilocks Zone" because orbiting outside the zone will make a planet either too hot or too cold for life: within the zone things are just right. Venus, for example, is roughly the same size as Earth, but being closer to the Sun its atmosphere is much hotter and consists primarily of carbon dioxide. The technical term is the Circumstellar Habitable Zone (CHZ) and is defined as the band around a star where liquid water can exist continually on the surface of a planet for billions of years. In the 1970s observers recognised that the increasing luminosity of the Sun means that its CHZ is slowly moving further away from it: meaning the Earth will eventually no longer be habitable. This is a reminder that even when other conditions are right, there is a window of opportunity for when life must make its appearance. We shall consider the role of time below.

The location of a planet is not only important with reference to its star, but also its position within its galaxy. Astronomers refer to the Galactic Habitable Zone (GHZ) which relates to factors such as the availability of the materials necessary to make certain types of planets and the presence of materials that can wipe out life. Further from the centre of the galaxy there are less stars formed because the density of gasses is lower. It is stars that provide most of the heavy elements in the galaxy which means the further out we go the decrease in metallicity. Here we are speaking from the viewpoint of someone who believes in galactic chemical evolution, something alien to the Genesis account of the creation of the universe, but in order to satisfy their arguments, I am demonstrating that even from within their paradigm, life in the galaxy is at least very rare. According to this thinking, the required amount of basic elements to make Earth weren't available in the Milky Way for a number of billions of years, and only then in its inner regions.

The second factor determining where life can survive in the galaxy is where it can survive long enough to become technological (again using the evolutionary paradigm). Life on any planet can be extinguished by impacts from large asteroids or comets, and also by radiation events. We are positioned where there are relatively fewer pieces of rock and ice likely to hit us, but also far enough away from the galaxy's centre where high-energy electromagnetic and particle radiation are emitted from the active galactic nucleus.

We now recognise that the existence of large gas giants like Jupiter and Saturn are also essential for our survival. Jupiter's gravity has removed most of the dangerous bodies from the asteroid belt that were hurtling through our region of space, Jupiter and Saturn have protected the inner Solar System from too many impacts: but simply having such large neighbours in our Solar System in itself is not enough. Many factors in Jupiter's formation could have prevented it from being any help to us. If it had formed a little earlier or later, had been larger or smaller, or had followed a different orbit, it could have failed to have absorbed the dangers to our existence. Asteroids have been important since it is thought by those who do not accept the Genesis account that they played a role in bringing water to the planet, but if their number was not controlled they could have extinguished life here. Once more we recognise a very specific set of requirements that are met by Earth to make it habitable.

Other features of Earth make it special too. The seasons only exist because our planet's vertical axis is at a tilt of twenty three and a half degrees. This means that we have variation in the temperature at any one place, without which there would be a reduction in how much of the Earth could be used for any kind of agriculture since some places would be continually too hot or cold. The size of the tilt is also important because if it were doubled then so too would be the temperature changes, making much of our land too hot in the summer and too cold in the winter. Once again, the Earth is just right.

Our orbit is also important, not all bodies around our Sun have such a regular movement. Earth's orbit is circular, but much of the Solar System we inhabit appears quite chaotic. Thankfully the larger planets are the least chaotic, but Mars, Mercury and Venus are surprisingly irregular in their movements. This is because the larger planets are affected mainly by the gravity of the Sun, while the smaller bodies are influenced more by the gravity of the larger planets than are their big brothers.

If the planet rotates around a larger star than our Sun (our star is smaller than many others) the annual orbit would take much more time and so affect the capacity for crops to grow and be harvested within a single cycle. This would also affect the duration of seasons, extending the warmer and colder periods. The duration of the day affects this too: if our days and nights were longer, the temperature differences between them would be much larger. An Earth-sized planet is very unlikely to follow a regular orbit if it is nearer the centre of the galaxy where its path will be affected by many sources of gravity. Though we have found other planets, so far they appear to have extremely eccentric orbits, making them unsuitable places for life to survive.

The number of galaxies in the universe is huge, but as we learn about them we are discovering how inhospitable to life most are. Ours is in the highest two percent in luminosity, meaning it is one of the most metal-rich galaxies that exist anywhere in the universe. The Milky Way is also positioned in a perfect location relevant to other galaxies: there are few other galaxies crowding us, which is vital for life. Other clusters of galaxies such as Virgo and Coma contain many more galaxies which leads to something astronomers call "galaxy harassment", when smaller galaxies can lose much of their gas to larger neighbours as they drift too close.

Earth's atmosphere is crucial for life to exist. Not just because of its mixture of oxygen and nitrogen but because it shields us from the billions of small meteors that strike the Earth every day. Our atmosphere doesn't just burn up meteors but protects us from the ultra-violet rays coming from the Sun which would otherwise harm us. As Guillermo Gonzalez and Jay Richards say, "Our atmosphere strikes a nearly perfect balance, transmitting most of the radiation that is useful for life while blocking most of the lethal energy."[5]

Within the Earth is a molten iron core which turns and so creates an electro-magnetic field that also protects us from the Sun's emissions. Without it we would not be alive. This core retains its liquid state partly because the Earth's crust is made up of tectonic plates that enable its movement. If the

Earth had any other kind of surface, it could not maintain a liquid iron core and its atmosphere would be stripped away. The magnetic field would decay after just a few hundred years, but the Earth regenerates its field, its structure acts like a vast dynamo that relies on a fast enough rotation to produce eddies in the outer core.

The magnetic field that protects us requires tectonic plates that enable the interior of the Earth to turn. One reason Earth is believed to have this feature is because of the continuous presence of liquid water on its surface. It may be remarkable to modern readers who have grown up with this understanding of our planet, that it was only in the 1960s that scientists were able to conclude that tectonics and continental drift is a reality. This is an example of a huge paradigm shift in scientific thinking as the old geosynclinal theory was discarded. Earth is believed to be the only planet in the Solar System that has plate tectonics; Venus for example has a thick crust that can not move.

It is not just the size of our neighbouring planets that is vital for life, the size of the Earth must also be within a narrow range for life to exist. If a planet is much smaller than Earth, its gravity will be weaker which would result in it losing its atmosphere too quickly, and the larger surface-area-to-volume ratio would create a cooler interior that wouldn't permit a sufficient magnetic field. It has also been observed that smaller planets are more likely to have chaotic orbits, as described above. If the planet is much larger than Earth however, the greater gravity would not permit the development of tall mountains and deep oceans, in fact many scientists suspect that the planet would be covered by the oceans if the planet became too large. It is important to remember that gravity increases much more quickly in proportion to planet size. So if the Earth was just twice its actual size, its gravity would be three and a half times greater because its mass would be fourteen times greater. A planet must once again be just right.

When we look at the night sky and see the extraordinary number of stars, it is easy to imagine life on the planets that orbit them. But despite Sagan's contempt for our star (he considered it very average) our Sun may be very rare. It is true that there are stars larger and smaller than our own, but contemporary science has begun to recognise some of the special qualities of the Sun. When astronomers talk about stars, the two basic properties they consider are its luminosity and its mass. While the Sun is in the mid-range, in reality only nine percent of all stars in the Milky way are as massive; most are what are called dwarf stars (M dwarfs). In fact over eighty percent of stars in the Milky way are low-mass red dwarfs which are unlikely to even have habitable zones. Only approximately four percent of all stars in our galaxy are what are called early G-type, main sequence stars like the Sun. In addition, the Sun is an extremely stable star, which means its output of energy only varies by 0.1 percent every eleven years (the period of a sunspot cycle). The Sun turns out to have a much smaller variation than most other stars, without which we would not have the stable climate we enjoy on Earth. Astronomers have also been able to calculate the amount of metals contained in the Sun and have observed that it is far richer in metals than other main-sequence stars of a similar age. This is vital for the formation of planets, since Earth for example is made almost entirely of metals. The Sun follows an orbit around the disc of our galaxy, and again we find that it is far more circular than that of other stars of a similar age. This is important because if our Solar System were to cross the spiral arm as others do, the vast molecular clouds there would reduce the likelihood of life surviving.

It is not only the stars we see in the night sky, but also our Moon. If we compare the rotation periods and angle of axis of Earth and Mars, we find them to be similar. But without the steadying influence of a large moon like the one Earth has, the tilt of Mars' axis wobbles; astronomers have calculated that the tilt of mars has varied from fifteen to forty-five degrees over a period of ten million years. Such changes prevent a stable climate and the growth of vegetation. In comparison, the earth's axis has moved no more than 2.5 degrees which not only ensures mild differences in our seasons but also protects the solar ice caps. The Moon's mass also creates sufficient gravity to produce ocean tides. If the Moon were much bigger however, its gravity could have slowed the earth's rotation which would result in a bigger difference between the temperatures of our nights and days. The moon is so crucial to life on Earth that Gonzalez and Richards went as far as saying:

The relationship between Earth and Moon is so intimate that it's probably best not to think of Earth as a lone planet, but as the habitable member of the Earth-Moon system. This partnership not only makes our existence possible, it also provides us with scientific knowledge we might otherwise lack.(6)

When we begin to study the stars and the nature of the universe we inevitably start to wonder at the nature of time. Astronomers use numbers to describe the age and distances from Earth that are so huge that the human mind is really incapable of grasping or imagining their reality. But even within such vast periods of time, there are specific periods when life is possible. This has become known as the *Cosmic Habitable Age* (CHA) because just as there are only certain places that are habitable, so too the conditions for life do not occur throughout all time. If we speak once more to the paradigm from which scientists work, believers in the Big Bang see the condition of the universe just after it came into existence, as having no stars and consisting of dense, hot plasma of elementary particles. At this stage, the heavy elements required to form human bodies had not yet been synthesised. The accepted understanding within astronomy is that it took a few hundred million years before stars came into being and began to eject life-essential elements. The size of the Milky Way means it has collected heavy elements more quickly than other, less massive galaxies. But this is not a process that will continue to make the universe more habitable, since the decline in long-lived radioscopes which are necessary for geology means there will be less habitable planets coming into being. We should note here that the old Pagan idea that time is cyclical was supported by the belief that the expansion of the universe may be slowing down, and that eventually it will begin to retract under the force of gravity. Scientists once argued that a continuous cycle of big bangs, expansions and contractions might be the nature of reality. However, new observations have confirmed that rather than slowing down, the expansion of the universe is accelerating. I mention this because it confirms a biblical sense of linear time, one that has a true beginning. It was Aristotle that argued that the universe is eternal, not Christians.

These are just a few examples from the very long list of requirements that make life on Earth possible according to the materialistic understanding of the universe. One of the main arguments employed to show that there must be life beyond Earth is the vast number of stars (and presumably planets) that exist. But this number becomes very small when divided by the factors necessary for life. Astro-biologists know this to be the case, but the insistence that the Earth cannot be the only place where life is found is not so much a mathematical or scientific issue, it is a philosophical matter. If alien life can be found, then God as the Creator of life can be forgotten, and with Him the moral framework that Christianity brings. SETI and its efforts to hear signals from another planet are the product of atheism. This is not to suggest that Sagan and others are trying to deceive us, they are not part of the deception of our title, but they are using the scientific paradigm of our age to try and justify their rejection of Christ.

Carl Sagan was mistaken when he claimed that with scientific advancement the possibility of finding extraterrestrial life would increase. The reverse is true, as our understanding grows, so does the realisation of how many factors it takes to make Earth habitable. This has always been the case, it is not a recent phenomenon. Kepler proposed that the craters of the moon were likely to be inhabited by aliens, and Percival Lowell interpreted the lines on the surface of Mars as being canals created by another civilisation. Sagan argued that just because life was made possible under the conditions on Earth, this does not mean that we should expect life to be limited to these kinds of environments. He fantasised about huge winged creatures that might be able to glide through the clouds of Jupiter. But as our knowledge of other planets in our Solar System has grown, so too has our conviction that it requires elaborate fine-tuning in physics and astrophysics to make a planet habitable.

The Copernicus Principle has been misused by many philosophers. Bertrand Russell sated that The Copernican Revolution will not have done its work until it has taught men more modesty

than is to be found among those who think Man
sufficient evidence of Cosmic Purpose.(7)

Much of the confusion comes from a modern misunderstanding of how people understood the universe before Copernicus made his observations. Again, there has been a popularisation of these errors which have become the accepted view of most people. The mistake is to imagine that geocentrism meant that the Earth's place at the centre of the universe gave special status. In fact seeing Earth's position at the centre was as a recognition of its heaviness, since things fall to earth from the heavens. This placed the earth near the bottom of the cosmos rather than the top, a place where things were corrupted and fallen. Copernicus was only able to come to an understanding of the Earth's movement precisely because he understood the Universe to be created by God and to have order and pattern which reflected the precision of mathematics. The belief that there is purpose to man's existence was seen to be undermined once it could be argued that our astronomical location was insignificant. But as scientific discovery challenges the first assumption, it is reasonable to question the metaphysical conclusion that follows it. If man is significant, it may be that rather than seeing the vastness of the Universe as empty and cold, we understood its purpose as supporting our existence and understanding of God. But Sagan and the other devotees of SETI base their view of life on Earth, and particularly that of man, on another theory

113

which they believe the discovery of aliens will prove: evolution.

Endnotes

1 – The term "Copernicus Principle" was created by Harlow Shapley (1885–1972) who in 1918 showed that the sun was displaced some distance from the centre of our galaxy, something he believed confirmed that the Earth and man have no privileged position or meaning.
2 – Astronomers have discovered a galaxy (called NGC 1052-DF2) that seems to contain very little dark matter.
3 – An example of this is the shifts in medical understanding of the body and the complete abandonment of paradigms as discoveries are made.

4 – Waltham, David, *Lucky Planet: Why Earth Is Exceptional--And What That Means for Life in the Universe,* Basic Books 2014   p. ix

5 – Gonzalez, Guillermo and Richards, Jay, *The Privileged Planet*, Regnery Gateway, Washington 2020 p. 66

6 – ibid. Gonzalez and Richards p.108

7 Russell, Bertrand, *Religion And Science*, Oxford University Press, New York 1961 p.222

Chapter Eight – The Theory Of Evolution

Throughout his writings, Carl Sagan repeatedly refers to evolution; of course, he refers to it not as a theory but as a fact. He is not alone in assuming this, given the right chemical circumstances, life will spontaneously come into being. As mentioned in the earlier chapter on SETI, the desire to find life beyond Earth is not driven by the recognition of the value of life, but a longing to prove that life itself is not unique to our planet and so not special, and so enable a challenge to the belief that it was created by God. But faith in evolution not only misrepresents the past, it creates hope in a fantasy of how man will be in the future. Future man can be portrayed as spiritually and morally superior, a creature so technologically advanced that through reason alone he will be able to understand the mysteries of the universe. Through his greater understanding he will overcome the limits of time and space and travel to distant stars. Once he has imagined himself this way, it is not such a big step to accepting that somewhere in the universe, some other form of life has already reached this level of evolution and made the trip to visit us. Evolution is the philosophy that makes belief in E.T.s possible, not just as aliens from outer space, but as a vision of our own potential future. After all, if aliens exist, there is no reason to assume that we were not the first, and so why shouldn't at least a few of them be ahead of us in the space race?

In fact there are many popular misunderstandings even about what evolution as a theory really is. Almost all of us have seen the drawing of man's progression from an ape to an upright Homo Sapien, and images like this can have a powerful effect on our consciousness, an effect that can go further than words. But even this image is misleading, suggesting an inevitable progression within evolution that those who believe in the theory do not all share. The former Harvard palaeontologist Stephen Gould makes it clear that to him evolution is a "meandering, directionless path marked by myriad "contingencies" and mishaps such as mass extinctions."[1] Gould is explicit in declaring that Darwin's theory did not elevate man to being the crowning glory of the evolutionary process, but to a position that is the consequence of purposelessness. As passionately as some astronomers use the Copernican Principle to declare that earth is nothing special, so the devotees of Darwin use his theories to claim the same about us.

The steady, inevitable increasing complexity and development of life through the process of evolution is just one popular misconception of what the evolutionists believe. As children we are exposed to cartoons and school text books that tell us that life started in the seas and developed lungs so it could crawl onto the sand and breathe air. From there it was just a matter of time before intelligent creatures like us showed up. But evolutionary theory is more than this, it is a philosophy that contradicts many scientific observations and must be understood if we are to grasp how and why so many intelligent people crave the proof of alien life.

Evolutionary Theory pre-supposes a lot about the beginning of life itself because as any honest biologist will admit, science can say very little about the origin of life from inorganic matter, let alone the move to complex life. While we may be able to list the necessary attributes for a planet to sustain life, such a list is not sufficient to bring life into being. There is an astonishing difference between chemistry and the biological information encoded in chemicals, and many biologists are admitting that life itself may be extremely rare, even if it did happen more than once. Darwin claimed that random variation and the effect of natural selection would give the appearance of a designer's hand being present in biology, he believed that chance events had fooled scientists of the past into seeing the appearance of design. Assuming life is without purpose, evolutionists are left to believe that life is an inevitable consequence, and so common throughout the universe, or a unique accident and very rare. But this false dilemma only works if we assume that there is no purpose to the universe or life.

When NASA declares it has found evidence of life on another planet, as it assures us it will, we must understand that what is identified as life may not be accepted as such even by all scientists. The definition of life is not as simple as we are led to believe. Most scientists recognise something as being alive because of what it does, whether this is to move, reproduce or react to certain stimuli. But there are examples of things that share at least some of these attributes but are not classed as living: the real feature that biologists look for is complexity. Where we see life, we discover a level of complexity that exceeds anything in the non-living world. Evolutionists claim that such complexity sprang from non-living matter by chance. Charles Darwin imagined how it might have come about, he wrote that proteins might have formed "In some warm little pond"(2) where they may have undergone changes which resulted in cells. But scientific knowledge about cells was extremely limited when Darwin suggested this, it was believed that simple chemical reactions would be enough to produce life. Today we understand that even in the most basic form of life bacteria (though viruses are simpler, they are not capable of independent existence), we see an extraordinary complexity of molecular activity coordinated to enable the cell to function. The complexity of life can, in biological terms, be summed up as information. Every living creature contains information. Most of us are familiar with DNA, the molecule of heredity that contains the code from which life is put together. The cell uses the information in DNA to structure life, but there is a problem with this discovery: where did the information come from? Though matter has many properties, information is not one of them. Biologists can offer no reason or law as to why DNA bases configure the way they do, and the likelihood of it happening by chance is far-fetched.

One of the great contributions to modern thinking about evolution made by Father Seraphim Rose was his recognition of two different strands of thought that are often presented as one; that is science and philosophy. He identified the core error in evolutionists' thinking which is to try to talk about evolution as though it has been proven by evidence, whereas he demonstrates that there is no such evidence that either proves or disproves evolution, there is only evidence that is interpreted according to the observer's philosophy.(3) Father Seraphim explained that when we identify variation in the animal kingdom, it is variation within a species; adaptation is not the same as evolution. He draws on the writings of St. Basil the Great to support this when he writes:

Let no one, therefore, who is living in vice, despair of himself, knowing that, as agriculture changes the properties of plants, so the diligence of the soul in the pursuit of virtue can triumph over all sorts of infirmities." No one, "evolutionist" or "antievolutionist," will deny that the "properties" of creatures can be changed; but this is not a proof of evolution unless it can

120

be shown that one kind or species can be
changed into another, and even more that every
species changes into another in an uninterrupted
chain back to the most primitive organism.
I will show below what St. Basil says on this
subject.(4)

Father Seraphim makes it clear that if God so willed that one species should change into another, it would not be something Christians could not believe, but simply that the scriptures and the Fathers of the Church teach that this is not the way God created us. Evolution is a product of modern thinking, it is a symptom of a change in man's perception rather than a conclusion that must be reached from the evidence. The Book of Genesis states that all creatures were made according to their kind, they did not become through a process of change from something else. Father Seraphim stresses that we are mistaken if we try to interpret the scriptures according to any scientific theory, but instead must accept the interpretation by the Holy Fathers, not least because science can fall prey to speculations such as evolutionary theory. This speculation is revealed to be in error most specifically when it speaks about the origin of man. While evolutionists will argue that we are the product of this random process of change, the scriptures and the Church Fathers describe a very different beginning. As St. Gregory of Nyssa writes:

The first man, and the man born from him,
received their being in a different way; the latter

by copulation, the former from the moulding of
Christ Himself.(5)

This is echoed by St. Cyril of Jerusalem when he calls Adam "God's first-formed man," but Cain "the first-born man."(6) And again in the writing of St. John Damascene who says:

The earliest formation (of man) is called creation
and not generation. For creation is the
original formation at God's hands, while
generation is the succession from each other
made necessary by the sentence of death imposed
on us on account of the transgression.(7)

Even amongst Orthodox Christians today there are some who choose a more allegorical interpretation of the Creation account in Genesis, but as Father Seraphim states, we are not free to choose how we wish to interpret the Holy Scriptures, but must accept the interpretations of the Holy Fathers. This is expressed by St. Ephraim who writes:

No one should think that the Creation of Six Days
is an allegory; it is likewise impermissible to
say that what seems, according to the account, to
have been created in the course of six days,
was created in a single instant, and likewise that
certain names presented in this account
either signify nothing, or signify something else.
On the contrary, one must know that just as
the heaven and the earth which were created in
the beginning are actually the heaven and the
earth and not something else understood under
the names of heaven and earth, so also

everything else that is spoken of as being created and brought into order after the creation of heaven and earth is not empty names, but the very essence of the created natures corresponds to the force of these names.(8)

Belief in Evolution is not scientific. This is a bold statement, but without observable evidence to support it, the theory does not satisfy the criteria necessary to be considered science. There has never been found a single piece of evidence for evolution from one distinct kind of organism into another. Even some evolutionists have acknowledged this. Jeffrey Schwartz, professor of anthropology at the University of Pittsburgh, stated that:

It was and still is the case that, with the exception of Dobzhansky's claim about a new species of fruit fly, the formation of a new species, by any mechanism, has never been observed.(9)

This may come as a surprise to those outside the field of biology, but it is a well-known fact amongst those who work within it. The reference to the fruit fly is based on the attempts by evolutionary geneticists to induce mutations in flies in order to create a new species; all attempts failed.

If evolution was a fact, it would not only have occurred in the past, but would be something observable in the world around us today. However, fossil records have never presented a single example of an intermediate, which is a species in the process of change. Julian Huxley, one of the main defenders of evolutionary theory in recent years, argued that we must move "our pattern of religious thought from a God-centred to an evolution-centred pattern."(10) This is the true goal of evolutionary theory, as Richard Lewontin of Harvard University openly admits:

We take the side of science in spite of the patent absurdity of some of its constructs, . . . in spite of the tolerance of the scientific community for unsubstantiated commitment to materialism. . . . we are forced by our a priori adherence to material causes to create an apparatus of investigation and set of concepts that produce material explanations, no matter how counterintuitive, no matter how mystifying to the uninitiated. Moreover, that materialism is absolute, for we cannot allow a Divine Foot in the door.(11)

The debate about evolution has moved on from how Charles Darwin imagined it. For him it was all about how life adapts to its environments and passes on those adaptations to its next generation.(12) Modern understanding of DNA has led many evolutionists to conclude that most evolutionary changes appear at the level of the genome and are essentially random and neutral. Darwin believed that through adaptation, species would steadily grow stronger and improve. Anything that was disadvantageous to survival would be removed through the process he called natural selection. By 1968, Motoo Kimura was arguing that in fact rather than being beneficial to the species, most mutations are neutral. Kimura observed that most changes offer no benefit to reproduction or survival, and so questioned the entire process of change that Darwin had postulated. Other biologists such as Jack Lester King and Thomas Jukes have since argued for what has become known as non-Darwinian evolution, and consequently evolutionists have become quite vitriolic in their defence of their own favoured form of evolution and rejection of the others. Developments in the understanding of DNA over the past fifty years have only added to the debate, and various theories combining the idea of selection with neutral mutation have gained popularity amongst many biologists. In making reference to this I am trying to demonstrate that the classic understanding of evolution taught in schools and reinforced through popular media, bears little resemblance to what evolutionists actually believe. Furthermore it is not a single, cohesive theory, but a collection of competing ideas that are rapidly dismissed as new ideas take their place. For evolutionists, this is the very nature of the scientific method, but it is important for us to understand that the myth of natural selection may still be popular amongst those without a scientific background, but for those in the field it is far from an agreed assumption.

A further danger of evolutionary ideas is that not just our physical being has improved, but that our mental and spiritual capacities are now greater than they have been in the past. But when we compare many features of contemporary popular culture with that of even a few hundred years ago, we immediately recognise a decline in both its intellectual and moral content. While the masses once followed the serialisation of Charles Dickens, today soap operas and the output of Hollywood distracts us with superficial and shallow amusements. The plays of the Ancient Greeks, let alone Shakespeare, have become barely penetrable to the average man who can no longer cope with the complexity of sentence structure and word play that entertained the Elizabethan masses. While our technology may advance, it is too easy to conclude that we must, as a species, be somehow more advanced than the people who went before us. But the reality is that the opposite is true. As the centuries have passed we have become spiritually duller; when the Church Fathers shared their divinely inspired understanding of the scriptures, it is hard to imagine that they could have foreseen the condition man's decline would lead him to. In *The Book of Genesis* we are told that God made all things good, but that as a result of human disobedience the whole cosmos fell from this condition. The introduction of death and disease as a result of sin and the harmful mutations that can cause further imperfections are signs of the degeneration of man; we also know that new pathogens and diseases are emerging as a result of mutation. Often those who argue that modern man is morally superior to previous generations will point to social changes, such as the end of slavery. But in fact there are, according to the United Nations, more people enduring slavery than there have ever been in any time in history. Similarly atheists will point to the "liberation" of man from traditional moral restraints on sexual behaviour, while in reality we are witnessing an increase in abortion rates and also the number of children being raised outside of a stable two-parent family.

None of this is purely academic. Our understanding of our origin directly determines who we are and our relationship to God. In his interview with Timothy Good, Howard Menger attempted to explain his encounters with aliens by suggesting that they might be advanced life forms from our own planet, he says:

One theory is that the Earth is the only one in the solar system which was given the gift of life, and this life developed a long time ago on this planet, and reached a civilisation far beyond ours, in technology and spiritual ideas.(13)

This perception that advancement in technology must automatically correlate with spiritual and moral development is entirely delusional. It is interesting to note that later in the same book Good quotes those who claim to have encountered aliens as describing them as "androgynous"; as we shall see, this peculiar idea that highly evolved beings should have indistinguishable genders conforms to Christian ideas about demons.

Though there are writers such as Vladimir Solov'ev and more recently Andrew Louth (in his book *Eastern Orthodox Theology*), who have embraced evolutionary theory as a means of trying to explain God's creation without having to accept the historical truth of the Genesis account, it was really the errors of the Enlightenment that have enabled the ideas to become so pervasive. The Enlightenment philosophers identified the rational, intellectual aspect of man as that which distinguished him from the rest of creation. Their reaction to the Protestant idea of Total Depravity (the belief that man cannot choose holiness because his very nature is corrupted) motivated much of their rejection of Christianity, however, Orthodoxy explains that the Protestant error lies in the confusion of nature with personhood, since choice is a function of the latter. But we would also point to Christ's incarnation: Christ has a human nature that was not different to ours, and we believe that He was entirely without sin. For the Orthodox, this means man's free will was never lost, and had the western philosophers of the Enlightenment been exposed to the Church's teaching, their reaction may have been different.

In response to the great silence that SETI has discovered in its search for alien life, some evolutionists have argued that we may be the subjects of a programme of study. It is called the Zoo Hypothesis and its adherents propose that technologically advanced E.T.s would avoid open interaction with us because they want to permit and study the natural evolution and sociocultural development of human life. It is an idea that has been developed by John Allen Ball, the former MIT Haystack Observatory scientist, in what is commonly known as the laboratory hypothesis. In this version the aliens not only observe us, but carry out experiments on us. The aliens in this scenario become the zoo keepers, but Ball insists that any experiments carried out on us would be for altruistic purposes only. As we shall see, those who have had direct contact with what they believe to be alien visitors have been subjected to experiences that reveal them to be anything but altruistic. Once more those who work within SETI are able to suggest hypothesis which are entirely without evidence, but are also beyond disproof. If the aliens remain hidden, then there can never be proof of their presence or activity. To this the evolutionists argue that the E.T.s must be waiting for us to evolve to a sufficiently acceptable moral, intellectual and technological stage before revealing themselves to us. The theory places Earth in a galaxy that is filled with intelligent lifeforms all operating according to agreed protocols when it comes to contact with primitive life such as ourselves. Other versions suggest a single lifeform might be more advanced and powerful than any of the others, and that the other E.T.s are required to submit to their command.(14) Reading these ideas quickly feels like popular science fiction, but without any criteria for validation beyond waiting for the disclosure to happen, those who believe in them are left in a state of perpetual anticipation. There are many examples, as we shall see, where those who have lived with this expectation turn to other means of satisfying their yearning, often in the occult.

There will be some readers who are rolling their eyes at how far-fetched some of this sounds. But this is not solely the realm of uninformed fantasists. In 2017 the Cambridge University Press published an online article entitled "Darwin's Aliens"(15) in the *International Journal of Astrobiology*. There readers were informed of how evolutionary processes might produce various forms of alien life. The article states:

Evolutionary theory can be used to make predictions about aliens. We argue that aliens will undergo natural selection – something that should not be taken for granted but that rests on firm theoretical grounds. Given aliens undergo natural selection we can say something about their evolution. In particular, we can say something about how complexity will arise in space.

What is noticeable is the way evolutionary theory is used to present expectations about the existence of alien life, not only as possible, but inevitable. Throughout the article the writers make constant reference to natural selection as the driving mechanism that must exist without God. For example:

We can ask, then, will aliens undergo natural selection? Evolutionary theory tells us that, for all but the most transient and simple molecules, the answer is yes. Without a designer, the only way to get something with the apparent purpose of replicating itself (something like a cell or a virus), is through natural selection.

Consequently, if we are able to notice it as life, then it will have undergone natural selection (or have been designed by something that itself underwent natural selection).

The article is filled with phrases such as "we can assume" and "our theories suggest", but as is entirely typical of this area of philosophy (it certainly is not science) there is nothing substantial in terms of evidence…because the evidence does not exist.

Even more than evolutionary theories, one of the reasons many people have accepted the possibility of alien visitors to Earth is our own exploration of space. But as we shall now see, NASA and the astronauts we are told have travelled beyond our atmosphere have themselves deliberately contributed to the E.T. explanation of UFOs.

Endnotes

1 – op. cit. Gonzalez and Richards, *Prvilidged Planet* p.286

2 – Darwin, Charles, Letter To Hooker, Cambridge University Library, Darwin Archives 1871

3 – Father Seraphim Rose explained this in his letter of response to the article "The Eternal Will" written by Dr. Alexander Kalomiros which was printed in *The Christian Activist*, Volume 11.

4 – St Basil the Great, In Homily V:7 of *The Hexaemeron*

5 – St. Gregory of Nyssa in his book his book *Against Eunomius*.

6 – St. Cyril of Jerusalem, *Catechetical Lectures*, II, 7

7 – St. John Damascene, *On the Orthodox Faith*, II, 30

8 - St. Ephraim, *Commentary on Genesis*, Chapter 1

9 - Mayr, Ernst, "Darwin's Influence on Modern Thought", *Scientific American* Volume 283, July 2000, p. 83

10 – Huxley, Julian, *Essays of a Humanist*, Harper and Row, New York 1964 p.222

11 – Lewontin, Richard, in his review of *The Demon-Haunted World*, by Carl Sagan in the New York Review of Books, January 9, 1997.

12 – This is the principle described by Charles Darwin in *On the Origin of Species* in 1859.

13 – Good, Timothy, *Alien Base*, Arrow Books, London 1999 p.260

14 – It is the principle behind Arthur C. Clarke's *2001: A Space Odyssey* (1968) and *The Sentinel* (1951) as well as the "Prime Directive" which is the rule in *Star Trek* that prevent s interference with any less technologically advanced alien life found on the travels of the Starship Enterprise. Within the stories, the Vulcans observed earth until humanity developed "warp drive", at which point Spock's race revealed themselves to us.

15 – Levin, Samuel, Scott, Thomas and Cooper Helen, "Darwin's Aliens", *International Journal of Astrobiology*, Cambridge University Press, 1st November 2017

Chapter Nine – NASA

On September 8th 2014, NASA convened a symposium at the Library of Congress to address the question of the likelihood of extra-terrestrial life. One of the chief organisers was the NASA/Library of Congress Chair in Astrobiology Steven J. Dick who declared in his presentation:

People just consider it more likely now
that we're going to find something – probably
microbes first and maybe intelligence later.
The driving force behind this is from a scientific
point of view that it seems much more likely
now that we are going to find life at some point
in the future.

During the two days that the meeting took place, similar assumptions were expressed by philosophers, Vatican theologians, scientists and historians, and their underlying theme was how to direct society into accepting the existence of alien life. Dick stated:

The idea is not to wait until we make the
discovery, but to try and prepare the public for
what the implications might be when such a
discovery is made.

Brother Guy Consolmagno, the then president of the Vatican Observatory Foundation, was fully behind this position. At the conference he declared:

I believe aliens exist, but I have no evidence. I would be really excited and it would make my understanding of my religion deeper and richer in ways that I can't even predict yet, which is why it would be exciting.

The message is one of change. One after another of the speakers reinforced the idea that a cultural shift must be manipulated into action in order to make people accept the existence of aliens. This shift, they argued, must be affected in every level of our culture: in entertainment, philosophy, science and, as Brother Guy so enthusiastically expresses, in theology. In the U.S.A. this change has already begun. A 2020 Ipsos poll reveals that a majority of Americans believe that there is life on other planets.(1) The poll revealed that fifty-seven percent of Americans believe there are intelligent extra-terrestrials, and forty-five percent believe that aliens have visited Earth. These figures are extremely high when we remember that, as Brother Guy admits, we have no evidence whatsoever to support these beliefs.

One of the reasons we might consider for this is the advances in technology, particularly in space flight. While the night sky has always been a source of fascination for man through the ages, only since April 12th 1961, when Russian cosmonaut Yuri Gagarin became the first person to leave Earth's atmosphere, has the reality of going beyond the boundaries of a planet been possible. Since then approximately five hundred people have looked back at the Earth from space, and this has been used by NASA to promote the expectation of travelling to other planets. In December 1968 the Apollo 8 mission was the first manned spacecraft to orbit the moon. It was on this trip that the famous photograph was taken of the Earth rising over the horizon of the moon, and the first time that man was able to see the Earth sitting in the darkness of space, and recognise how the whole of human life existed on that single planetary globe that appeared so fragile. It is interesting to note that the three crewmen experienced intense realisations making this trip: while Bill Anders who took the photograph abandoned his Roman Catholic faith, Frank Borman and Jim Lovell became convinced of a greater reality beyond the physical universe; as we shall see, the effect of being in space has profound effects on nearly all astronauts. The British astronomer Fred Hoyle famously predicted in 1948 "once a photograph of the Earth, taken from the outside, is available… a new idea as powerful as any in history will be let loose." He was right.

NASA has taken to talking about the discovery of E.T.s with the same confidence that Steven Dick expressed. On August 7th 2014, on their official website they stated:

New approaches and new technology for detecting sentient beings elsewhere suggest that there is good reason to expect that we could

uncover evidence of sophisticated civilizations –
the type of aliens we see in the movies and on TV
– within a few decades.(2)

Beneath this outlandish claim, the astronomer Seth Shostak outlines NASA's reasons for believing in such beings:

NASA's Kepler spacecraft, launched in 2009 to
survey our region of the Milky Way galaxy,
identified a large number of Earth-sized planets
outside our solar system where conditions
could potentially permit the presence of life as we
know it. Inside our solar system, new
information about Saturn's moon Enceladus, has
spawned speculation about possibilities of
life there. The same with Jupiter's moon Europa.
And, in 2015, NASA announced strong
evidence that liquid water flows intermittently on
present-day Mars.(3)

We see here the difference between what NASA hopes to find, and the way it is presented to the public. Even the most optimistic astrobiologists do not anticipate meeting Vulcans or Klingons or anything like them living on the planets and moons of our solar system. While the exaggerated rhetoric might excite the public, it is microbes or some form of basic life that is hoped for in the quest to disprove the special nature of life on Earth.

Shostak proceeds to claim that there are tens of billions of what he calls "Earth-cousins" that have been discovered in our galaxy in the last five years, and in a moment of clarity he says of life elsewhere, "if there isn't any, there's something really exceptional about what's happened here on Earth." He acknowledges that there is no scientific data to suggest that what happened on Earth isn't exceptional, but it is clear that such a conclusion is philosophically unacceptable to him. This is the basis for all SETI activity, unlike all other science that produces a hypothesis and seeks to prove or refute it with evidence, Shostak admits:

SETI is not like that. The hypothesis is that there's somebody out there as clever as the average resident of Virginia Beach — but there's no way to disprove that. You can't prove they're not there.(4)

NASA has been involved with the issue of UFOs for over sixty years, and from the very beginning they were focussed on controlling public perception. In 1960 the U.S. government had a report made on the potential impact of alien contact with Earth. It was carried out by the Brookings Institute for NASA and produced a document entitled Proposed Studies on the Implications of Peaceful Space Activities for Human Affairs.(5) Chief amongst its findings was that the American public should be prepared for the psychological impact of alien encounter. In order to survive such an event, even in 1960, the proposal was to change the way people live and think. The report says:

Anthropological files contain many examples of societies, sure of their place in the universe, which have disintegrated when they have had to associate with previously unfamiliar societies espousing different ideas and different

138

life ways; others which have survived such
an experience did so by paying the price of
changes in values and attitudes and behaviour.(6)

The Brookings Report covered a wide range of topics and was particularly focussed on space travel, the issue of extra-terrestrials is covered within this context. However, NASA has completed a more recent report called "Would contact with extra-terrestrials benefit or harm humanity? A scenario analysis".(7) Here NASA concludes that the disclosure to the public of alien life would be in conflict with religious belief. They state:

If ETI (Extra Terrestrial Intelligence) do exist
within the galaxy, then confirmation of their
presence would have profound implications for
human science, philosophy, religion, and
society. ...Some people might consider mere
detection to be harmful to humanity. These
people include those with religious perspectives
and other worldviews that depend on the
idea of humanity (and Earth-life more generally)
playing a unique and privileged role in the
universe. The detection of ETI could challenge
these worldviews and therefore be perceived
as harmful by those who hold such beliefs.(8)

The important point to note is the philosophical assumption that any religious belief that presumes that life on Earth is unique will inescapably be challenged by the encounter with life from elsewhere which NASA assumes is inevitable. But more than this, not even encounter is necessary for

139

such calamity for religious belief, the mere detection of such life will be enough. Meanwhile the aliens themselves may be portrayed as the true saviours of humanity. The report states:

An advanced ETI may be capable of solving a great many of humanity's problems, such as world hunger, poverty, or disease. Benevolent ETI may even design their first message to contain information on how to avoid technological catastrophe in order to help less developed civilizations succeed. From humanity's perspective, this is the best-case scenario for ETI contact.(9)

This is a theme we will consider in more detail in a later chapter. Similarly the report questions whether alien visitors might be "pure energy beings that lack physical form, and even residents between multiple universes" which is another topic we will focus on in detail. While suggesting Abrahamic religious beliefs may have to change, the NASA report expresses the idea that alongside technological development the aliens may also be spiritually evolved to a point where "They may have taken up transcendental spiritual practices that focus their efforts inward rather than outward." While this may be nothing more than the conjecture of someone excited by their fantasies about E.T.s, it does reveal the theological assumptions at work amongst those producing the report.

Before considering the statements made by astronauts, we must remember that as participants

140

in the most expensive scientific project in the history of the world, every comment and article they produce will be carefully scrutinised and approved by NASA. With so much money at stake, and a reliance on politicians recognising sufficient public support to continue the funding, astronauts are not permitted to make comments that might damage the organisation's interests. Therefore, when Edgar Mitchell, the sixth astronaut said to have walked on the moon, claims that the U.S. government has covered up the truth about aliens being in contact with them for years, we can assume that NASA considers it advantageous to their efforts to allow him to do so. A growing interest in UFOs does nothing to harm public support for space exploration, and NASA may simply be using Mitchell's statements to promote their own cause; but Mitchell has been on the fringes of conventional science in other areas too. He claims that a Canadian psychic named Adam Dreamhealer cured him of kidney cancer. However, Mitchell admits that he never had a biopsy proving he had cancer in the first place, but had a sonogram and MRI that indicated what might be consistent with cancer.

Edgar Mitchell is not the only astronaut to have endorsed belief in UFOs. Dr Brian O'Leary (1940 - 2011) went on to become Physics Professor at Princeton. He stated:

There is abundant evidence that we are being contacted, that civilisations have been monitoring us for a very long time. Their appearance is bizarre from any type of traditional materialistic western point of view. That these visitors use the technologies of consciousness, they use toroids, they use co-rotating magnetic disks for their propulsion systems, that seems to be a common denominator of the UFO phenomenon.(10)

O'Leary says a lot in this short statement. But again it is first necessary to consider his wider views and involvements. After what he claims was a remote viewing (psychic) experience in 1979 and a near-death experience in 1982, he became fascinated with the concept of how technology and consciousness overlap. He became a public supporter and gave lectures on what became known as Religious Science, and once more we see that the religions in question are non-Christian: he gave talks for the Sivananda Yoga Vedanta Centres and the Unity Church which promotes Transcendentalism. This gives us some understanding of his comment about what he perceives as "western" and "traditional", and his claim that their observation of humanity has been going on for a long time subtly reinforces his claims about the aliens being more advanced than ourselves. The intimate knowledge he claims to have about UFO propulsion, if true, could only come from official studies of craft. That he would be permitted to reveal secrets kept from the public is odd, and suggests NASA and other government agencies are happy to have such ideas circulated regardless of whether they are true or not.

Gordon Cooper (1927 – 2004) an astronaut from Project Mercury (the first manned U.S. space programme) has an explanation. He argues:

In my opinion I think they were worried it would panic the public so they started telling lies about it. And then I think they had to tell another rile to cover their first lie, now they don't know how to get out of it. Now it's going to be so embarrassing to admit that all these administrations have told so many untruths, it would be embarrassing getting out of it.
There are a number of extraterrestrial vehicles out there cruising around.(11)

Cooper dismissed rumours that he had encountered UFOs while on NASA missions, but did claim to have witnessed one while flying over Germany in 1951. In his autobiography *Leap Of Faith*, he even claimed to have sent a roll of film containing pictures of a flying disc that had landed on an air base, to military intelligence, but received no follow up investigation into what had been seen. Amongst UFO believers, Cooper is often quoted as a strong source of evidence for their existence. But many of his stories do not stand up to close scrutiny. For example, he claimed that his Gemini 5 space capsule was repeatedly struck by meteorites which left deep gouges in its outer shell. But the capsule can be examined, as it is on display in Houston: it shows no signs of any such impacts and the NASA ground crew could see no indication of impacts when it returned from its flight. The sad truth is, Cooper experienced a string of business failures after leaving NASA, and it seems that as he turned to his heroic past as a source of validation he began to expand on the factual realities of what had happened. In his autobiography he even described meeting with engineer Wendell Welling in Utah, to see a flying disc that had been built. He describes the experience this way:

I sat at the control station about ten feet away. The sole 'flight control' was an airplane-type stick... The only noise in the room was the slight whir of the generator. I applied gently backward pressure on the stick, and the saucer jumped off the test stand, soundlessly, and rose into the air effortlessly to ten feet or so... I flew the saucer for about ten minutes, and the experience really opened my eyes to what a vehicle of this configuration would do, specifically, the tremendous lift that could be developed from the saucer shape. Boy, I thought, we've been going the wrong way all these years with winged aircraft.(12)

When the book was published it generated a huge reaction amongst UFO researchers, but Gloria Welling, Wendell's daughter, tells a different story. In an interview with James Oberg, a retired space shuttle Mission Control specialist, she said she was present when Cooper visited and that no such test flight ever took place.(13) As a witness we might wonder whether Cooper's accounts of UFOs are any more reliable, but NASA allows the tales to be told.

We should note that while some astronauts have used their fame and the credibility their work brings them to further fringe ideas, others have embraced Christianity. Jim Irwin of Apollo 15 became a Protestant preacher, and Charlie Duke of Apollo 16 became a committed Christian, saying the sight of the Earth in space confirmed in him a realisation that our existence could be no meaningless accident.

It is not only ex-astronauts that perpetuate the idea of extra-terrestrials. On 3rd December 2018 Sean Keach reported in a U.K. newspaper(14) that NASA scientist Professor Silvano P. Colombano had stated that aliens may already have visited Earth, but that their physical nature may be so different to ours that we are unable to detect them. Revisiting the idea of evolution, Colombano is quoted in the article as saying that civilisations much older than our own could have developed technology so advanced that we are unable to imagine what it is like. He stated:

Considering further that technological development in our civilisation started only about 10,000 years ago and has seen the rise of scientific methodologies only in the past 500 years, we can surmise that we might have a real problem in predicting technological evolution even for the next thousand years, let alone six million times that amount.(15)

The Professor makes reference to "higher technologies" and his comments are filled with words such as "could", "possibly", "may" and "likely"; in short, his statements about the likelihood of alien life are once more based on no evidence, only assumptions.

In American culture, and to some extent that of all western countries, astronauts achieved the status of heroes. The scientific achievements of NASA are celebrated as confirmation that mankind is still progressing and achieving great things. But we must take a more critical view of the organisation if we are to understand its pronouncements about UFOs in a more objective way. NASA is often presented officially as a civilian agency, which creates the idea of scientists working independently to discover scientific truths. But in reality NASA collaborates with the CIA, the Department of Defence, the National Security Agency and a number of other agencies. Many NASA personnel are issued with high level security clearances and many of the reports that NASA produces are exempt from public disclosure. In 1978 the White House made NASA its official mouthpiece on all topics relating to UFOs, which is a clear indication that it is far from independent. Many of NASA's projects are directly funded from the defence budget, and all films produced by NASA are screened by the National Security Agency before they can be seen by the public.

NASA officially came into being in response to the Soviet Union's October 4, 1957 launch of its first satellite, Sputnik I. The true story extends to the closing days of the Second World War when rocket engineer Wernher von Braun was taken to the U.S.A. to help develop America's weapon design. Von Braun had been responsible for the creation of Hitler's V2 missiles that killed approximately five thousand civilians in British cities; many concentration camp slaves were employed in the manufacture of these missiles. Von Braun died in 1977, but even before his death there were many who believed he should be tried as a war criminal.(16) In fact, he became director of development at the U.S. Army Ballistic Missile Agency in Huntsville and was handsomely rewarded by the U.S. authorities for his work. Von Braun was just one of about a hundred and twenty scientists that instead of being imprisoned for their service to the NAZIS, were given passage to America in exchange for their engineering skills as part of what was called *Operation Paperclip*. The Soviet Union also took German scientists into their research and development facilities. It was Von Braun who was the head of the team that developed the Saturn V rocket that carried the Apollo Eleven mission to the moon. In a 1958 Time Magazine article questions were raised about Von Braun's switch of loyalty from the NAZIS to the U.S, to which he responded: "Once the rockets are up, who cares where they come down? That's not my department."(17)

Not all NASA employees have been so keen to support the idea of alien visitors. When reports emerged in the press that astronaut Scott Glen had not only seen but photographed UFOs from the Mercury 7 capsule on 31st May 1952, he went to great lengths to deny it. So outraged was he that claims were being made that any such sighting occurred, he began to publicly criticise reports of any other astronauts having had such experiences. In November 1972 he even wrote to other astronauts asking them to confirm that they had not encountered UFOs on their missions, and James Lovell responded in writing stating:

I have to admit that during my four flights into space, I have not seen or heard any phenomena that I could not explain...I don't believe any of us in the space program believe that there are such things as UFOs.(18)

Despite all this, there are organisations which persist in promoting the UFO agenda, not least the United Nations. In 1978 Gordon Cooper was invited to speak at the Special Political Committee of the United Nations General Assembly in order to present his theories about UFOs. His experience as an astronaut was considered to give his opinions great validity, and there was widespread reporting of his comments about advanced civilisations visiting Earth. Of course, Cooper's questionable comments about other topics were not raised. Despite the claim by UFO researchers that the mainstream media only presents negative stories about their beliefs, the reality is that extravagant headlines sell newspapers, and combining the word "NASA" or "astronaut" with a headline about UFOs gives a story greater credibility.

One such example is the "Black Knight" theory. On 4th December 1998, NASA launched its first Space Shuttle mission (named STS-88) to the

International Space Station (ISS). During the week-long flight a photograph was taken which included a dark object in orbit around the Earth. It was quickly identified as a piece of debris left by a previous mission, and ex-NASA employee and now journalist, James Oberg was able to determine that it is most likely a thermal blanket. But stories quickly spread on the internet that what had actually been pictured was an ancient extraterrestrial artificial satellite. Theories developed and a range of unrelated observations were conflated to support the alien explanation. It is claimed that scientist Nikola Tesla had first heard broadcasts from the satellite, and in 1960 remains of an Air Force Discoverer VIII satellite were at first mistaken for a Russian spy satellite, but believers claim that this too was a sighting of The Black Knight. When the photographs were released in 1998, many newspapers reported the story of a possible probe left here to monitor Earth, but the originator of the story, Scottish author Duncan Lunan, who had first speculated on its alien nature in 1973, admitted his theories were unsound. Despite this, a quick search of the internet provides countless examples of sites where The Black Knight story continues to be treated as truth. Distrust of NASA has reached such a level on these sites that no evidence that can be given will ever persuade believers that NASA is not issuing disinformation to hide the truth of its origin.

Such distrust of NASA is not entirely without foundation. The scientists there have made a number of extremely unwise decisions. For example in 1958 NASA planned to detonate a nuclear bomb on the moon. Known as Project A119 (also known as A Study of Lunar Research Flights) the U.S. Air Force wanted to demonstrate its technological prowess to the Soviets, and NASA scientists agreed that a nuclear explosion on the lunar surface would do the job. The consequences were completely unknown, and thankfully NASA was prevented from carrying it out. The military links continue to this day. Although the Space Shuttle missions have ended, a miniature unmanned version called the X-37B Spaceplane continues to fly, but the public has never been told what it is doing in space.

In 1973 the crew of Skylab 4 mission decided to mutiny. So unhappy were they with the way they were being treated by ground control that they turned off all communications and refused to co-operate for a day. After re-establishing contact the crew made demands about their work schedule and ground control conceded to their demands. This demonstrates something of the culture within NASA.

In 1999, NASA launched the Mars Climate Orbiter, a hugely expensive satellite intended to study the atmosphere of Mars. But after travelling to the planet, instead of taking up its orbit the craft crashed into its surface. The error was simply that the scientist who programmed the flight control software had calculated the engine thrust in the wrong units (English pounds instead of metric newtons). I include this detail as a reminder that when NASA makes unsubstantiated claims about the inevitability of encountering extraterrestrial visitors, we must put their comments into context. NASA employees have been drawn, at least historically, from morally dubious backgrounds, individual astronauts have been shown to be lying about their experiences, and NASA scientists are capable of being both unwise and incompetent – like the rest of us. They do not make public statements based solely on scientific evidence, but are one organisation amongst many competing for government funding. Without a single piece of evidence to support their conclusions, they are not to be treated as the authority on the nature of UFOs. Their opinions are based on personal philosophies, beliefs and interests, and many of these include not just non-Christian teachings, but some that are overtly anti-Christian.

Endnotes

1 - Ipsos Poll can be found at https://www.ipsos.com/en-us/news-polls/majority-believe-intelligent-life-exists-on-other-planets

2 - Aug. 7, 2017 MEDIA ADVISORY 17-018 found at https://www.nasa.gov/langley/feature/when-will-we-find-et-and-what-happens-if-we-do

3 – ibid. Shostak, Seth

4 – ibid.

5 – The entire report can be read here http://www.nicap.org/papers/brookings.pdf

6 – ibid.

7 – The report can be found as a pdf here https://arxiv.org/abs/1104.4462

8 – ibid.

9 – ibid.

10 – O'Leary, Brian, *Miracle in the Void: Free Energy, UFOs and Other Scientific Revelations*, Mass Market Paperback 1996

11 – Cooper, Gordon, interviewed in the documentary *Out of The Blue* which aired on the Sci-Fi Channel on June 24th 2003.

12 – Cooper, Gordon, *Leap Of Faith*, HarperCollins 2001 p.266

13 – Interviewed for *Space Review*, May 1st 2017 the original article can be found at https://www.thespacereview.com/article/3228/1

14 – Keach, Sean, *The Irish Sun* 3rd December 2018, article can be viewed here https://www.thesun.ie/tech/3468812/nasa-admits-tiny-super-intelligent-aliens-may-have-already-visited-earth-and-says-some-ufo-sightings-cannot-be-explained-or-denied/

15 – ibid. Professor Silvano P. Colombano

16 – Such as from Wayne Biddle, a Pulitzer Prize-winning journalist and author of *Dark Side of the Moon*

17 – *Time Magazine*, February 17, 1958 | Vol. LXXI No. 7

18 – Letter to Scott Carpenter from James Lovell, 12th December1972. Reproduced by Timothy Good in *Above Top Secret*, p.376

Chapter Ten – Close Encounters

The encounter with what are interpreted as aliens is very often an unsettling experience that creates fear, insecurity and a longing to understand the meaning of the event. In many accounts there may be physical sensations of weakness and emptiness, and for many people who claim to have had contact with aliens, the long term result is often depression. Though the "aliens" often use positive words such "salvation" and "rescue", what is communicated is often threatening, and for those who have repeated encounters, the threats become part of a demand for submission.

Encounters are normally divided into six types, a system of categorisation devised by Dr .J. Allen Hynek (who had spent time reviewing UFO reports while working on Project Bluebook). His categories first appeared in his 1972 book The UFO Experience and subsequently became the standard terminology for differentiating UFO experiences. The most common is simply seeing lights in the sky at night, which he classed as the first category. The second category is the same as the first except that sighting takes place in daylight. This was the category in which he placed the typical flying saucer and cigar sightings. The third group is those that are confirmed through independent radar sightings.

Most UFO sightings fall into these first three categories and the typical response is puzzlement and sometimes excitement. The other categories are different in that they involve what Hynek called "Close Encounters", and it is to these that many witnesses have profound emotional and psychological reactions. The first of these next three, Close Encounters of The First Kind, are when what is thought to be an alien vehicle is seen to land or come near to people. Witnesses describe experiencing intense reactions that often last a long time. Close Encounters of The Second Kind are similar to the previous category except that some kind of physical mark or trace is left behind, or there is interference with electrical or communication systems nearby. The category also includes those cases where there is a physical impact on humans or animals, such as temporary paralysis, or even the apparent healing of wounds or sores on the skin. Many people who have experienced these kinds of encounters also report finding strange marks left on their bodies.

The final category, Close Encounters of The Third Kind, is when beings are encountered who are believed by witness to be the occupants of the UFO. When Steven Spielberg made his film of the same name, he used Hynek as a technical consultant. Of all the types of sightings, this final group creates the most difficulty even amongst

UFO researchers. On a number of occasions Hynek himself admitted that for the sake of the credibility of his work he wished this category did not exist, but believed that to ensure scientific objectivity, it was necessary to include it. It is the strange and sometimes contradictory nature of these encounters that make serious UFO researchers uncomfortable. But the sheer number of cases has meant they cannot be excluded: Dr Jacques Vallee (who we shall consider in more detail later) claims that of the cases he has personally investigated and catalogued, more than three hundred of them involve the appearance of some kind of humanoid creature. He also claims that of these three hundred cases, at least one third involved multiple witnesses.

As we will see, the kinds of experiences interpreted as alien encounters have been understood differently according to the culture and beliefs of the witnesses. For example in 1088, Shen Kuo wrote the *Dream Pool Essays* which includes a passage titled "Strange Happenings". Here we read of a strange orb that he claimed visited the Chinese city of Yangzhou. Kuo writes:

It opened its door and a flood of intense light like sunbeams darted out of it, then the outer
shell opened up, appearing as large as a bed with a big pearl the size of a fist illuminating the interior in silvery white. The intense silver-white light, shot from the interior, was too strong for human eyes to behold; it cast shadows of every tree within a radius of ten miles. The

spectacle was like the rising Sun, lighting up the
distant sky and woods in red. Then all of a
sudden, the object took off at a tremendous speed
and descended upon the lake like the Sun
setting.(1)

Here we see how the enraptured witness seems almost enchanted by the effect of the light and remains focussed on the physical manifestations of what is happening. But even enthusiastic believers in the benign nature of UFOs have to acknowledge that the effects of these encounters can be harmful. Timothy Good reproduces a report from an eyewitness of a UFO incident in 1955 which states that as light was emitted from the UFO:

I suddenly seemed to be pushed over, and I fell
down in the snow with my bicycle on top of
me. What is more, I could not get up again.
Although the bicycle only weighs a few lbs it
seemed as though an unseen force was holding
me down…I felt rather dizzy, as though I had
received a near knockout blow on the point
of the chin.(2)

Being knocked to the ground is a relatively mild effect compared with the psychological and spiritual impact UFOs have on other people's lives. In a later book Good details the effects of a different witness who was told by the beings that he would suffer a heart-attack:

Bobby was affected deeply by his experiences.
Sometime in the spring of 1963 he did indeed
suffer a heart attack…Although no further
contacts ensued, he told me that from the end of

1962 to July 1964, the extraterrestrials communicated with him by means of images, projected on to the mirror of his room in the house in Bechenham…the images seemed to be generated by, or projected from, a red light in the sky…Within a circular image of about one foot in diameter, a face was seen and a voice heard. The discourses were mainly philosophical…Bobby believed that most people who have the "rare privilege" of witnessing "strange beings or visions from other planets" suffer from depression…others can be driven to the point of madness or suicide.(3)

We must note that these disturbing effects are recounted in a work by someone extremely sympathetic to the acceptance of UFO visitations as something beneficial for humanity. The description matches the symptoms of both mental ill-health and the consequences of becoming involved in the occult. Later Good goes on to relate other frightening encounters which he admits reflect "an increasingly sinister trend" in the events surrounding close encounters.(4) He tells of a young mechanic living in Brazil who was followed by a shining disc containing beings of around fifty centimetres in height, looking like chubby dwarfs with slit eyes. In his account, the young mechanic says he was "Overpowered: all energy and will-power drained out of him as he was drawn towards the lights." Once he had been forced inside the craft he claims that seven of the creatures examined him, and that they appeared to communicate telepathically. They then dumped him at the side of the road where he lay watching them fly away. Later at the hospital:

Paulo was examined by Dr Munir Bussad, who found the patient to be in a state of severe nervous shock. He had an abnormally fast pulse-rate, badly scratched and bruised arms, his eyes were badly bloodshot and he was unable to see properly.(5)

The doctor reported that the witness was familiar to him and had no history of mental illness. When he was questioned by police five days later he still could not see properly and kept breaking down into tears. His bouts of weeping continued for some time. As is often the case in these accounts, the victim reported further visitations by the same creatures.

The sinister trend that Good refers to reflects a common perception amongst many observers. Christopher Bader, writing about the "UFO Contact Movement" in the U.S.A. notes that "The first claims of extended contact with alien beings in the early 1950s were entirely different in form and content from the current, frightening UFO abduction tales."(6) Just as individual contactees often describe an increasingly threatening and disturbing nature as multiple encounters are experienced, so too the collective experience of these events has become more negative. It was in the 1960s that contactees started to report aggressive aliens who forced their victims to accept medical procedures. Witnesses of this kind began to be called abductees. Bader summarises the common features of such experiences as follows:

In a prototypical UFO abduction account, the victim, or victims, sees a strange object far away in the sky. The object comes closer and closer. Suddenly the person blacks out and has no recall of the following events. The next thing that person remembers is looking at a clock and realizing that a couple of hours have passed that cannot be accounted for. Troubled by this memory gap or "missing time" as it is called in UFO circles, the victim may undergo hypnosis or other therapies to attempt to remember this period of time. While under hypnosis the victim recalls that strange, alien beings took him or her aboard their ship, submitting him or her to an exhaustive and often painful physical examination. The victim is then released with little or no memory of the event. Most UFO abduction researchers believe that the "aliens" somehow erase the victims' memory of the abduction.(7)

Many of these details were first reported by Betty and Barney Hill whose experience of abduction in 1961 set the pattern for what would follow. They later wrote an account of what they claimed had happened to them which made them a considerable amount of money.(8) Neither of the couple could account for anything that had happened to them during their lost period of time, and it was only under hypnosis that they were able to describe the events. While sceptics point to the differences in details recounted by witnesses of single events, such as in the case of the Hills (she claimed the aliens spoke English while he said they had no mouths) this may be the result of the beings deliberate creation of confusion. Certainly the physical appearance of aliens has been a growing cause of disagreement amongst researchers, bringing some to conclude that many races of aliens may be visiting earth. Up until the 1980s, the religious nature of the alien messages was also a cause of ridicule amongst those examining abductees' accounts, and only with the growth of the New Age movement has there been a readiness to embrace a "spiritual" interpretation of what the visitors are doing and saying. As we shall see, this has certainly been the case for those promoting the UFO agenda such as Dr Stephen Greer.

In 1987, Walt Andrus, director of the Mutual UFO Network, the United States' largest UFO research organization, claimed that after studying thousands of UFO reports, he had been able to identify four main types of UFO occupants. He broke them down as a small humanoid, an experimental animal, a human-like entity, and what he called the "robot". Andrus' categories assumed great authority amongst UFO researchers, to the extent that those cases that conformed to these descriptions began to gain greater publicity, while those of different beings were generally classed as hoaxes. What is clearly at work is a desire for credibility amongst UFO researchers. This small, exact group of alien visitors may feel more believable than the huge number of different beings described by witnesses. From tall, blonde humanoids, to hairy dwarfs, child-size "greys" and many others, the visitors have presented themselves in such a way that often those who are trying to understand their experience are met with ridicule even from amongst others who say they have had encounters. The consequence can be isolation and confusion.

A further change in understanding about close encounters has been the shift from single events to multiple encounters. Until the late 1970s, the common understanding was that a person was lucky or unlucky enough, depending on your perspective, to be involved in a UFO incident because they happened to be in a particular place at a certain time. This has been replaced with the belief that aliens identify certain people and not only observe them, but repeatedly intervene in their lives. The idea developed from the work of Budd Hopkins, author of many books including *Missing Time: Documented Stories of People Kidnapped By UFOs And Then Returned With Their Memories Erased*. In this book Hopkins explored the case of Virginia Horton who had multiple encounters with the greys, who Hopkins believed had inserted some kind of probe into their victim's body in order to track her. It was Hopkins who introduced into U.S. popular culture the idea that aliens are conducting some kind of breeding programme with humans, or are removing genetic material for their experiments. He has observed that many abductees

162

have suffered emotional and psychological trauma as a result of these procedures, and concluded that the aliens were entirely indifferent to the experiences of human beings.

In the past few decades many abductees have claimed to have suffered intrusive procedures that have seemed sexual in nature. David Jacobs, Associate Professor of History at Temple University, supports Hopkins' ideas and says:

No matter how they handle the experience, all abductees have one thing in common: They are victims. Just as surely as women who are raped are victims of sexual abuse or soldiers can be victims of Post-Traumatic Stress Disorder, abductees are victims who require sensitivity and, if needed, help in understanding what has happened to them and the possible consequences that abductions have had for their lives.(9)

It is not only the personal impact on individual witnesses that has suggested there may be something dangerous behind the UFOs, aeroplanes have been affected and pilots have lost their lives. On 7th January 1948, Captain Thomas Mantell in his P-51 Mustang jet pursued a UFO. Two miles from Franklin, Kentucky he was killed when he crashed. The official report first claimed that he had been chasing the planet Venus, and this story was changed to him mistakenly pursuing a weather balloon. Though pilot error was the official verdict, Captain Mantell's final words over the radio were: "It appears to be a metallic object...tremendous size...I am trying to close for a better look."(10)

This is not an isolated incident. In 1953 the former Commanding General of Air Defense Command General Benjamin Chidlaw said, "We have stacks of reports of flying saucers. We take them seriously when you consider we have lost many men and planes trying to intercept them."(11) One such incident took place on 23rd November 1953 when an F-89 was sent to investigate an unknown object over Michigan. The jet's crew of two, Lieutenant Felix Moncla and Lieutenant R.R. Wilson, located the object and as they approached the ground radar reported that the two craft converged and then disappeared. No wreckage or bodies were found and no explanation was ever given to explain the event.(12)

In the past twenty years there has been a growing movement promoting the idea that despite the negative experiences of abductees in the past, contemporary encounters are not only positive, but bestow some kind of spiritual blessing on the one who encounters the visitors. Betty Andreasson has been a key writer and proponent of these ideas, preferring to call those who have encounters "experiencers" rather than abductees. She has helped to produce a handbook for those who have encountered aliens, assuring them that once they have overcome their shock and fear, great personal development and improvement is possible as a result of the event. Together with John Salter, Chair of American Indian Studies at the University of North Dakota, Andreasson has established the small grey alien as the accepted norm of how aliens appear, and the two writers have been the driving force behind the cultural shift to believing aliens are here to watch over us and help us advance both spiritually and technologically.

However, amongst secular sociologists and psychologists a range of observations are beginning to be made about the phenomenon of alien encounter that suggest the traditional understanding, even from a secular perspective, is far from the whole story. Researcher Lucas Tromly has observed that abduction is an almost entirely American experience, and that even within the borders of the United States, it rarely happens to people of Asian ethnicity.(13) For sceptics this is only more evidence that the reports are nothing more than fantasies produced by a particular culture. While there may be some substance to this for some or many reports, the evidence suggests there may be another explanation. As support groups have become more common amongst people suffering many different kinds of experiences, researchers have begun to identify the similarities between UFO abductions and occult experiences. Robert Sheaffer has written extensively on the parallels between abductions and witchcraft, noting that both can involve non-human creatures, uncovered memories, and bizarre sexual activity.(14) Perhaps the most disturbing connections have been described by Gwen Dean who has described forty-four parallels between alien abduction and satanic ritual abuse.(15) She recognised that for both victims of abuse and alien abduction, there are suppressed memories that reveal the experience started in childhood, they involve the entire family and are said to occur generationally. Dean also noted that the examination table where abductees often describe undergoing intrusive procedures mirror the satanic altars used in ritual abuse. For non-Christian writers the conclusion is that the production of the UFO memory is how the victim's mind has coped with the trauma of the abuse. While this may be the case for some, as we shall see, it does not explain them all.

Christopher Bader describes how the accounts of both abductees and ritual abuse survivors "exhibited a strikingly similar combination of the quasi-religious and psychotherapeutic" elements.(16) He also notes that in both cases the victims are predominantly female (sixty-three percent), and either the victim or someone close to them will have been involved in what he describes as a "New Age" religion or activities linked to them such as astrology. Bader also observes that victims of both experiences often exhibit similar distrust of revealing what has happened to them: ritual abuse victims because they fear reprisal from the cult, and abductees because they often believe a conspiracy involving the government is suppressing information about UFOs. Despite the popular myth that abductees are uneducated "simple country folk", Bader discovered that of those he was able to question through support groups, sixty-three percent of those claiming to be abductees have a college education.(17) He says:

The author had a strong impression from reading the personal stories of abductees and ritual-abuse survivors, viewing their documentaries, and attending their meetings, that their ranks were primarily composed of highly educated, white females. The survey findings merely confirm that impression.(18)

He found that on average, abductees claimed to have been visited ten times, and though he recognised that support groups used to consider what the "aliens" had done to them as akin to rape, many were now trying to find a way to understand their experiences in a positive way. Despite this, however, many find their marital and employment circumstances disrupted because of feelings of victimhood, suspicion and an obsession with conspiracy theories. From a secular, therapeutic perspective, it makes sense that it is the personality type that should lead to claims of these kinds of experiences. But we must also acknowledge that deeply traumatic events will result in similar effects on people's personalities, and that dismissal of these kinds of claims, however fantastical they may appear, may be to miss some underlying reality that may not be explained either by visitors from outer space or an over-active imagination. Bader himself acknowledges how committed the victims are to their claims, and how deeply these stories have become rooted in their lives. The level of psychological disturbance alone would indicate

167

something has happened to them. As we shall see, the Church Fathers reveal to us that the answer is neither psychological nor extra-terrestrial, but spiritual.

End Notes

1 - Kuo, Shen, *Dream Pool Essays*, Metro Fifth Avenue Press, LLC 2014

2 – op cit. Good, Timothy, *Above Top Secret* pp. 448 -.449

3 – Good, Timothy, *Alien Base, The Evidence For Extraterrestrial Colonisation Of Earth*, Arrow Books Ltd 1999 pp. 318 -319

4 – ibid. Good, p.449

5 – ibid. Good, p.450

6 – Bader, Christopher, "The UFO Contact Movement From the 1950s To The Present" *Studies In Popular Culture*, Volume 17, Issue 2, 1995 p.74

7 – ibid. Bader, p.79

8 – Hill, Betty and Barney, *The Interrupted Journey: Two Lost Hours Aboard a Flying Saucer*.

9 – Jacobs, David, The Threat: Revealing the Secret Alien Agenda, Simon and Schuster; Reprint edition 1994 p.257

10 – Analysis of Flying Objects Incidents In the US, Air Intelligence Division Study No. 203, Directorate of Intelligence and Office of Naval Intelligence, Washington DC, 10th December 1948

11 – op cit. Above Top Secret, Quoted by Timothy Good, p.265

12 – ibid. Good, p.266

13 – Tromly, Lucas, *The Journal of Popular Culture*, Vol 50, No 2, 2017, p.276

14 - Sheaffer, Robert. "A Skeptical Perspective on UFO Abductions." In: Pritchard, Andrea & Pritchard, David E. & Mack, John E. & Kasey, Pam & Yapp, Claudia. *Alien Discussions: Proceedings of the Abduction* Study Conference. Cambridge, North Cambridge Press, pp. 382–88

15 – Dean presented her findings at the Alien Abduction Conference held June 13–17, 1992, at MIT in Cambridge, Mass.

16 – Bader, Christopher, "Supernatural Support Groups: Who Are the UFO Abductees and Ritual-Abuse Survivors?" *Journal for the Scientific Study of Religion* Blackwell Publishing, p.669

17 – ibid. Bader, p.675

18 – ibid. Bader, p.676

Chapter Eleven – Jacques Vallée

In the 1977 film *Close Encounters Of The Third Kind* the director Spielberg had François Truffaut play the character of Lacombe, an all-knowing scientist whose understanding of how the extraterrestrials communicate is pivotal to the story. Lacombe was based on the Frenchman Jacques Vallée (born 1939) who has been a hugely influential figure in both the study and perception of UFOs. Vallée has been at the forefront of computer science, he was involved in how the internet took shape, and he is an astronomer who made a good living through private equity investments; but he is most famous for his writings on UFOs. It was through his work that UFO research earned a greater credibility, and as we shall see, he has been one of the key promoters of what has become known as the interdimensional hypothesis.

His early work, in 1963, was focussed on the computerised mapping of the surface of Mars at the Paris Observatory, which quickly gained him a professional reputation. But he had already had some success under the name of Jérôme Sériel, his pseudonym for his science fiction writing that earned him the Jules Verne Prize in 1961. It was when he moved to Chicago that he came under the influence of J. Allen Hynek who was the chair of the Northwestern University's astronomy department where Vallée was employed. Vallée's own interest had begun when he witnessed a UFO in 1955. He also claims that while working on the staff of the French Space Committee in 1961, they began tracking a satellite orbiting in the opposite direction to the earth's rotation, something human technology could not achieve at that point. He says that he witnessed the tapes that recorded this incident being destroyed by his superior, and that this led him to conclude that the UFO story was being covered up.

Vallée's technical expertise enabled him to write about UFOs(1) in a way that convinced many other scientists of the legitimacy of the subject. At first he supported the conventional idea that UFOs were visitors from other planets, what is known as the Extraterrestrial Hypothesis (ETH), but as his research continued, Vallée began to question how far this explanation could account for the various UFO phenomena that were being reported. By 1969 he had become convinced that something very different was happening, what he called the Multidimensional Visitation Hypothesis. Vallée had come to recognise that the behaviour of UFOs, the way they appear and disappear, the speed and changes in direction and the changes in their shape and size, could not be explained by the theory that the aliens simply possessed technology that is more

171

advanced than our own. He proposed that UFOs were evidence of beings that exist beyond time and space, allowing them to be amongst us at any moment of their choosing.

At the time there was great disapproval amongst other UFO researchers who not only rejected Vallée's new theories, but also recognised that their cause had lost one of its most credible voices. However, many contemporary researchers, such as Dr Steven Greer, have now embraced his ideas. Vallée has continued to develop this theory and in 1990 wrote a paper explaining why the ETH was not an adequate explanation of UFO reports. He says the five principle reasons are:

Unexplained close encounters are far more numerous than required for any physical survey of the earth; the humanoid body structure of the alleged "aliens" is not likely to have originated on another planet and is not biologically adapted to space travel; the reported behavior in thousands of abduction reports contradicts the hypothesis of genetic or scientific experimentation on humans by an advanced race; the extension of the phenomenon throughout recorded human history demonstrates that UFOs are not a contemporary phenomenon; and the apparent ability of UFOs to manipulate space and time suggests radically different and richer alternatives.(2)

As is often the case for those who become involved with UFO research, Vallée has also focussed on a number of esoteric areas of enquiry, he has written arguing that many religious visions may be attributed to UFO encounters(3) and during the 1970s and '80s he was a consultant for the CIA's Stargate Project which was research into remote viewing. While supporting the reality of UFO encounters, Vallée argues that what people are encountering is a non-human form of consciousness that is able to manipulate time and space. He acknowledges that this consciousness has been deceiving humanity throughout the ages in order to manipulate us into serving its own goals. He also believes that many people have experienced staged UFO encounters intended to develop a social acceptance of the idea of extraterrestrials in order to undermine traditional religious beliefs. This, he argues, is another form of deception that is simultaneously taking place: enacted by governments and international bodies who encourage the perception that governments are concealing evidence of aliens and UFOs in order to maintain the myth and contribute to confusion.

In his book *Dimensions*, Vallée sets out his beliefs, he says:

Although I am among those who believe that UFOs are real physical objects. I do not think they are extraterrestrial in the ordinary sense of the term. In my view they present an exciting challenge to our concept of reality itself.(4)

For Vallée the reality being challenged is our social, cultural and religious assumptions that are the framework from which we experience life. He writes:

173

In my view, the widespread belief among researchers of the field in the literal truth of the "abductions" is only a very crude approximation of a much more complex tapestry. Another reality is involved here. A reality characterized by cosmic seduction, strange signs in heaven, and paranormal events that present a rich panoply of psychic phenomena.(5)

Like so many people attracted to this topic, Vallée not only predicts a radical shift away from traditional religious belief, he seems to delight in it. He proposes:

Faced with the new wave of experiences of UFO contact that are described in books like Communion and Intruders and in movies like Close Encounters of the Third Kind, our religions seem obsolete. Our idea of the church as a social entity working within rational structures is obviously challenged by the claim of a direct communication in modern times with visible beings who seem endowed with supernatural powers.(6)

Having stated that the beings behind UFOs appear to be deceiving us, he remains willing to embrace the appearance of these supernatural beings as those who will free humanity from the constraints of out-dated religions. An error many people can fall into is the belief that all spiritual experiences must be good simply because they are called "spiritual". We have witnessed a growing acceptance in the use of psychedelic drugs to attain "spiritual" insights and visions as people look to other cultures and belief systems, and underpinning it all is the assumption that there is truth and goodness in the experiences. In fact many saints have warned that the immediate realms of existence beyond our conscious experience are filled with danger, for reasons we shall explore later. Vallée makes the same kind of mistake about UFOs, he says:

Let us start with a simple fact: man has always been aware that he is not alone. All the traditions of mankind carefully preserve accounts of contact with other forms of life and intelligence beyond the animal realm. Even more significantly, they claim that we are surrounded with spiritual entities that can manifest physically in ways that we do not understand.(7)

Vallée is making a direct assault on the religious interpretation of these beings. Any talk of angels, demons or even God, is now to be seen as a primitive misinterpretation of the UFO phenomenon. He claims that only with our modern level of technology has our cultural and emotional nature been ready to cope with this new paradigm. He re-interprets biblical events from this new perspective, seeing Ezekiel's vision as a UFO abduction, and even St Anthony of the Desert's visions are given a UFO explanation.(8) Regardless of how the individuals involved in these events were able to describe and explain them, Vallée adopts the modern arrogance of knowing better, and believes he is able to correct what he considers the errors of the saints. Vallée has correctly

175

identified the truth when he writes "a close parallel exists between modern claims of UFO contact and age-old traditions that involved alien spiritual entities"(9) but his mistake is in understanding which interpretation is correct: as we shall see, there is a great deal of evidence from the writings of the Church Fathers and various saints that these encounters have been happening for a long time, and that their true nature has been explained to us. But attempting to dismiss Christian teaching, Vallée misrepresents the Church when he says "Christian theology does not have much to say about the angels",(10) a false statement that is intended to suggest that the visitation of angels is merely a misinterpretation of UFO encounters by people who do not have any real sense of even angels themselves. In fact the Church has a highly developed understanding of angels based on the angels' own words and also a number of prophetic visions. Acknowledging that the Orthodox Church does have icons and writings concerning angels, Vallée has decided that this material is purely symbolic, and that a literal interpretation of them indicates UFOs: of course he chooses not to recognise the explanations given by those who wrote them.(11) But Vallée also recognises that the details surrounding these events does not support the possibility that extraterrestrials are the answer, he writes:

However strong the current belief in UFOs from space, it cannot be stronger than the Celtic faith in the elves and the fairies, or the medieval belief

in lutins, or the fear throughout the Christian
lands, in the first centuries of our era, of
demons.(12)

Vallée recognises that modern man is living through a time when a new form of folklore is developing around UFOs, one that he believes is as mistaken about the true nature of UFOs as he believes were the old traditions of the Church. From a Christian perspective we can see that both his own conclusions and those of the typical UFO believer are simply two sides of the same error, one based in the assumption that a modern perspective must somehow be closer to the truth than those of the past. But he is correct in recognising the importance of what is happening, as he states:

This is not simply a case of a few tales relating
encounters between a few humans and
strange creatures from the sky. This is an age-old
and worldwide myth that has shaped our
belief structures, our scientific expectations, and
our view of ourselves.(13)

It is important beyond the conclusions we draw from it, since our understanding of these phenomenon is crucial in the way we both understand and react to them. Accepting false beliefs leaves us vulnerable to many dangers, as we shall consider later. Vallée is right when he says "to control human imagination is to shape mankind's collective destiny",(14) since a rejection of Christian truth in favour of modern myths exposes us to more confusion and lies. It is this impact on culture and society that Vallée is most interested in, and without arriving at the same conclusions as Christian observers, he correctly notes that:

it is possible to make large sections of any population believe in the existence of supernatural races, in the possibility of flying machines, in the plurality of inhabited worlds, by exposing them to a few carefully engineered scenes the details of which are adapted to the culture and symbols of a particular time and place.(15)

The development of the UFO myth has drawn on the contemporary status of our scientific knowledge and cultural anxieties in a way that was not possible at any other time in our history. As we shall see, the deception that lies at the heart of this is not random or without purpose, but is aimed at faith in God. An important part of this deception has been a growing occult feature in the encounters. As Vallée confirms:

During the 1970s, the report of paranormal events in connection with close encounters with UFOs seems to have become the rule rather than the exception, and most investigators have found it very difficult to deal with this aspect of the cases because it does not match their expectation of what an extraterrestrial visit would be.(16)

This is not the only feature which confirms the Orthodox Christian understanding of UFOs, but Vallée's own philosophical preconceptions leave him unable to reach the conclusions of the Church, despite him being able to recognise the links. He acknowledges the bizarre and confusing aspects that accompany UFO sightings, but is always willing to assume wise and benevolent motives for what is happening. In many cases the so-called extraterrestrials say or act in deliberately confusing ways. Witnesses have been instructed to build machines that have no purpose, or have been presented with contradictory statements, and under the intense emotional impact of the experience, the need to explain the event has led many people to mental ill health. The technique of presenting an unsolvable question is often used in advertising, it is a psychological trick that distracts the mind from making reasoned evaluation; but as has been stated earlier, it is also known to be a means of making the mind more vulnerable to hypnosis. Vallée reveals a lack of consistency in his approach when he states that such absurdities are to be interpreted as symbolic rather than literal, the exact opposite of how he argues Orthodox theology should be understood. He insists:

When a witness meets a UFO occupant who asks, "What time is it?" and replies, "It's 2:30," only to be bluntly told, "You lie – it is 4 o'clock" (this actually happened in France in 1954), the story is not simply absurd. It has a symbolic meaning beyond the apparent contradiction of the dialogue. Could it be that the true meaning of the dialogue is "time is not what you think it is," or "any measurement of time can only be relative"?(17)

179

Without the Orthodox perspective Vallée applies the thinking of various occult groups such as the Cabala to explain these semantic absurdities, believing them to have the nature of poetry and containing esoteric truths. But in his desire to apply a positive interpretation he is willing to overlook the obvious; that the description and interpretation by the witness may sometimes be correct. He therefore rejects any Christian viewpoint, such as when he writes:

In fact, some witnesses have thought they had seen demons because the creature had the unpredictability and mischievousness associated with popular conceptions of the devil.(18)

Once more the simple truth is staring him in the face, but he is unable to see it. He even states the truth without being able to understand what is being said, he says:

anyone who has examined the beliefs of esoteric groups could not fail to note similarities between certain UFO encounters and the initiation rituals of secret societies.(19)

His recognition of the links between what he considers as an "opening of the mind" within occult rituals and UFO encounters conforms to Orthodox understanding, but Vallée's error is in imagining that they are of benefit to anyone. He considers changes in consciousness as equivalent to spiritual realities, but fails to ask why other forms of consciousness should desire the praise of human beings. He writes:

The phenomenon originates with entities that manipulate our reality and our destiny for their own purposes. Using our naïveté and our lack of critical judgement in the presence of "miracles," these entities, in this view, play with our emotions in order to be worshipped as gods.(20)

As if quoting directly from the writings of Father Seraphim Rose, Vallée concludes that UFOs will be the basis of new belief systems:

I think the stage is set for the appearance of new faiths, centered on the UFO belief. To a greater degree than all the phenomena modern science is confronting, the UFO can inspire awe, the sense of the smallness of man, and an idea of the possibility of contact with the cosmic.(21)

We must be clear that this statement is not only an expression on how profound Vallée believes the UFO encounter to be, but is his summary of what accounts for the religious beliefs that already exist. Vallée rejects any possibility that those who claim to have had encounters with God, angels or demons might be in a better position than he to account for their experiences, and uses the UFO phenomenon as an argument for the materialistic nature of existence. He presents lists of features of both miracles and UFO encounters(22) to demonstrate that the two are really the same kind of event, never for a moment imagining that the beings who he admits create confusion and absurdity might be capable of imitating the acts of God.

181

Vallée makes other useful observations, such as the fact that there are simply too many UFO encounters for them to be alien visitors: this was also one of Carl Sagan's objections. If UFOs really were visitors from very distant planets, their appearances would be incredibly rare, but sightings by reputable eye-witnesses continue in large numbers. Vallée makes the claim that potentially there have been millions of UFO events in the past two decades alone.(23) Such numbers make the extraterrestrial explanation untenable. Similarly the appearance and disappearance of UFOs points to something other than space vehicles, and the medical experiments that abductees claim to have endured are less sophisticated than even our own present medical practices. Vallée's conclusion is correct when he says "I propose that there is a spiritual control system for human consciousness and that paranormal phenomena like UFOs are one of its manifestations".(24) But his willingness to recognise this control as the means to our spiritual development and the advancement of our worldview leaves him and anyone who accepts his theories, vulnerable to deception. Vallée welcomes the changes that UFOs bring because they offer mankind a realisation of a "higher destiny", he celebrates the happiness that UFO witnesses have found as "the next form of religion, with a new spiritual movement",(25) but does not question the ultimate value or purpose of these states of contentedness.

Vallée insists that the psychological and emotional impact that UFO encounters have on people indicate a physical reality, and that the neurological changes are signs that there is some kind of technology at work, but he is more concerned with the social and cultural impact than where it leaves the individuals. He recognises that many cults that have formed as a result of UFO encounters often have elitist attitudes, and his focus on the social dynamic causes him to overlook the creation of pride and suspicion of others that witnesses frequently develop. From a Christian perspective, the spiritual sickness that UFO encounters can create is far more serious than the kinds of politics that predominates amongst UFO groups. He considers the case of one of the earliest contactees, George Adamski, and talks at length about how the CIA and other political groups were manipulating Adamski's stories for their own ends, but does not focus on Adamski's involvement in Theosophy. In the same way Vallée does not consider Whitley Streiber's involvement with Gurdjieff's mystical philosophy as important, and at no point questions whether an earlier involvement in occultism may have left someone vulnerable to UFO encounters.(26)

Vallée might be forgiven for not recognising a causal relationship between spiritual events, but not that in pursuit of evidence to support his theories he misrepresents religious belief. For example, in his book Wonders in the Sky: Unexplained Aerial Objects from Antiquity to Modern Times he and his co-author Chris Aubeck select sections of The Mithras Liturgy, a Greek papyrus found in Egypt, to make it appear that it is a UFO being described; in fact the text makes no such allusion.(27) The same approach is applied to biblical texts, using misinterpretations of a number of commonly understood images (such as the chariot of Ezekiel) to propose the idea that the encounters with angels and signs from God were no more than UFOs. His errors often result from his dependence on second hand sources rather than the ancient texts themselves.

Vallée does, however, raise a number of issues that we must try to understand: the degree to which government agencies have deliberately used the UFO myth for their own purposes, the degree to which science fiction has contributed to the modern mind-set that is willing to embrace the UFO myth, but now let us focus on the inter-dimensional reality that many UFO researchers are now beginning to believe in.

Endnotes

1 – Vallée, Jacques, *Anatomy of a Phenomenon: Unidentified Objects in Space – a Scientific Appraisal* NTC/Contemporary Publishing. 1965 and *Challenge to Science: The UFO Enigma* – with Janine Vallée, NTC/Contemporary Publishing, 1966

2 – Vallée, Jacques, "Five Arguments Against the Extraterrestrial Origin of Unidentified Flying Objects", *Journal of Scientific Exploration*, 1990

3 – Vallée's work includes *Messengers of Deception: UFO Contacts and Cults*, And/Or Press, 1979 and *Wonders in the Sky: Unexplained Aerial Objects from Antiquity to Modern Times*, Tarcher, 2010.

4 - Vallée, Jacques, *Dimensions, A Casebook of Alien Contact* "Introduction: Closed Minds, Open Questions", Anomalist Books 2014

5 – ibid. Vallée, Jacques, p.iv

6 – ibid. Vallée, Jacques, p.v

7 – ibid. Vallée, Jacques, p.8

8 – ibid. Vallée, Jacques p.12

9 – ibid. Vallée, Jacques p.20

10 – ibid. Vallée, Jacques p.23

11 - ibid. Vallée, Jacques p.23

12 - ibid. Vallée, Jacques p.45

13 - ibid. Vallée, Jacques p.62

14 - ibid. Vallée, Jacques p.85

15 - ibid. Vallée, Jacques p.86

16 - ibid. Vallée, Jacques p.90

17 - ibid. Vallée, Jacques p.94

18 - ibid. Vallée, Jacques p.94

19 - ibid. Vallée, Jacques p.100

20 - ibid. Vallée, Jacques p.111

21 - ibid. Vallée, Jacques p.114

22 - ibid. Vallée, Jacques pp.114-116

23 – ibid. Vallée, Jacques p.135

24 - ibid. Vallée, Jacques p.141

25 - ibid. Vallée, Jacques p.150

26 - Whitley Streiber is the author of *Communion*, in which he describes his claim to have been repeatedly abducted by extraterrestrials.

27 – In "The Introduction" to Wonders in the Sky: *Unexplained Aerial Objects from Antiquity to Modern Times*, Tarcher Perigee 2010

Chapter Twelve – Inter-dimensional Beings

Jacques Vallée understood that UFOs cannot be nuts-and-bolts vehicles, however advanced they might be, because they do not conform to the physics of how objects move. He is not alone in this observation, and as we shall see, even those researchers who believe in the extraterrestrial theory have had to acknowledge that the behaviour of these "craft" is beyond conventional explanation. It is an important point, because only when the myth of alien spaceships has been debunked can their true nature be understood.

Timothy Good's sober analysis has made him one of the most respected UFO researchers around the world. His books document the evidence for the belief that Earth is being visited by aliens. But even Good is forced to recognise that the phenomenon has features which indicate something more. One of these is the way UFOs are seen to change shape. Good quotes the case of a BOAC flight in 1954 on which Captain James Howard reported seeing such an incident. The commander's report says:

The large object was continually, slowly, changing shape, in the way that a swarm of bees might alter its appearance.(1)

This account was given by a highly experienced pilot who is clearly not describing a space vehicle. Good provides a number of such examples. In the skies above Tehran in September 1976 the Iranian Air Force fired rockets at a UFO seen by many observers on the ground. The missiles had no effect, and a second UFO appeared and somehow merged into the first. Later a third object emerged from the first and fell to the ground at a great speed. The witnesses anticipated an explosion, but instead the UFO gently struck the ground and filled the surrounding area with light.(2)

Good is one of a growing number of researchers having to create theories about UFOs moving between dimensions to account for what is being observed. He quotes the French scientist Dr Pierre Guerin who stated:

Scientists are not only embarrassed by UFOs: they're furious because they don't understand them. There is no possibility of explaining them in three-dimensional space-time physics.(3)

The same conclusion was reached by the U.S. Air Force which analysed thousands of sightings. Dr Carl Jung, the Swiss psychologist, noted that in these reports something other than spaceships was to be found, and concluded:

The American Air Force (despite its contradictory statements), as well as the Canadian, consider the observations to be real...However, the discs do not behave in accordance with the physical laws but as though without weight, and they show signs of intelligent guidance.(4)

Jung had much more to say about UFOs, and we will consider his writings in more detail later.

As an honest researcher, Timothy Good admits that the extraterrestrial hypothesis has been rejected by CIA special study groups and stated that

Even though we might admit that intelligent life may exist elsewhere and that space travel is possible, there is no shred of evidence to support this theory at present. There have been no astronomical observations in confirmation – no slightest indication of the orbiting which would probably be necessary – and no tracking.(5)

The French researcher Aime Michel observed that such elements of UFO encounters only add to what Vallée described as absurdities. Michel called them "a festival of absurdities", resisting all rational attempts to categorise them,(6) and contemporary science continues to fail to provide a definitive explanation of what the UFO phenomenon is about. Eyewitnesses describe objects that are too small to be vehicles that have performed interstellar journeys, they are able to alter their movement along lines of trajectory and accelerate and decelerate in ways that defy the theory that they are some form of technology.

Brad Steiger, an Iowa college professor, has made a detailed examination of the "Blue Book" files compiled by the U.S. Air Force. In his many books he has concluded that the phenomenon is one of beings that are multi-dimensional, but rather

189

than coming from other planets, he argues that they originate from Earth.(7) Steiger's ideas have gained favour with both Hynek and Vallée who have come to support what is known as *Indigenous UFOs*. In order to accommodate these ideas writers such as John Keel have extended theories about interlocking universes which, he believes, also account for other psychic phenomenon such as poltergeists. Although Keel identifies himself as an agnostic, he talks of an invisible world that surrounds and affects us, one that is full of delusion and manipulation. To the Christian reader this all sounds familiar, and indeed Keel refers to what he considers as outdated ideas of demons as being an unsophisticated interpretation of the events. We might observe that one of the crisis of our contemporary age is that men are once more becoming aware of demonic activity, but no longer have the Christian framework from which to understand it.

Jacques Vallée states it clearly when he says "To put it bluntly, the extraterrestrial theory is not strange enough to explain the facts."(8) Though he maintains that UFOs are some kind of physical objects, the inter-dimensional theory is his only way of accounting for their behaviour while insisting on a materialistic explanation. He produces a circular argument, seeing UFOs as the proof of other physical dimensions, and using this as the explanation for UFOs themselves: they become both the evidence and the key. He uses the term "multiverse" which he believes is the only way to account for the psychic aspects of the phenomenon. His conclusion becomes more alarming when he claims that humanity is powerless before beings who "masquerade" as Martians and angels and primitive gods (Vallée considers visions of the Theotokos as part of the same deception). To the horror of his co-believers (Vallée continues to be the "outsider of the outsiders" as he likes to put it) he proposes that:

The UFOs are physical manifestations that simply cannot be understood apart from their psychic and symbolic reality. What we see here is not an alien invasion. It is a spiritual system that acts on humans and uses humans.(9)

It is interesting how often Vallée makes statements that could sit comfortably alongside those of Orthodox Christian writers, and yet he continues to fail to make the connection between what he recognises and what has been explained for two thousand years. He even risks acknowledging that what might be called miracles are beginning to be accepted by modern physics, since there are events that violate what were once thought to be the laws of space and time. In such a universe, he speculates, beings may be free to travel between planets without the use of spacecraft. He acknowledges that physicists such as Dr Michio Taku and Jennifer Trainer are recognising that for the theory of the big bang to be true, there would have to be at least five dimensions in existence.(10) Of course, anything outside of our universe cannot be proven to exist (and a lack of testability makes it unscientific) and so such theories are a matter of belief: or faith! This is nothing new, Hugh Everett and John Wheeler of Princeton University argued the "Many Worlds Interpretation" of quantum mechanics as far back as 1957, and physicists have pondered what were called "superstring" theories since the 1970s, arguing for many more dimensions. These kinds of intellectual pursuits draw close to spiritual truths when they begin to use the language of chaos and entropy, though claiming that free action is no more than an illusion.(11) This is important because we must recognise that these theories are not spiritually neutral, they do not exist in a separate realm of thinking from religious belief, but form the foundations from which claims about human nature and the existence of the cosmos are made. Vallée complains that physicists do not see the consequences of recognising that energy and information are the same thing, and concludes that the theory of space and time is a "cultural artefact". This accounts for his repeated reference to UFOs manipulating society and culture, since he believes that this is their true purpose.

Vallée's background in computer programming has made a deep impression on his perception. While this may be said of many influences in our lives, for him it leads to a dangerous rejection of God's action in the world, he states:

The synchronicity and coincidences that abound in our lives suggest that the world may be organized like a randomized data base (the multiverse) rather than a sequential library (the four-dimensional universe of conventional physics).(12)

This leaves human beings stumbling through life, trying to grasp reality through association, just as computers find key words or files, and Vallée proposes that it is this that accounts for both miracles and UFOs, and eradicates the irrational since we are no longer trying to fit events into any sequential reality. The reality of cause and event is no longer required to exist in our universe, and UFOs can then be understood as events occurring beyond what is perceived; either the cause or event may occur elsewhere. This then removes the necessity of a Creator God, since the limits of time within our cosmos are no longer true limits at all, and the possibility of eternal existence rather than an eternal God makes the big bang a product of a cause that can never be investigated: a matter of faith not science.

Once more we see these kinds of theories invariably lead to the occult. Vallée says:

The subject invites many troubling, fundamental questions. If energy and information are related, why do we only have one physics, the physics of energy? Where is the physics of information? Is the old theory of magic relevant here?(13)

Vallée concludes that the link between psyche and matter is the answer to the UFO question. He determines that what is required is an abandonment of traditional ways of thinking in favour of "creative speculation". The inherent dangers of the imagination have been explained by many Church Fathers. In Orthodox thinking, the imagination is at the edges of consciousness, and is where demonic activity can have its greatest influence on us. Within such an approach, Vallée expects human beings to experience not only encounters with UFOs but other typical psychic and occult events. He writes:

I propose to define consciousness as the
process by which informational associations
are retrieved and traversed. The illusion of
time and space would be merely a side effect
of consciousness as it traverses associations.
In such a theory, apparently paranormal
Phenomena like remote viewing and precognition
would be expected, even common, and
UFOs would lose much of their bizarre
quality.(14)

Vallée believes that this change in human consciousness is a step forward in our evolution. UFOs are simply part of the process by which unknown beings are attempting to help us advance, what he considers "part of the control system for human evolution". While claiming that we do not know what it is about us they are interested in, and despite the evidence for their far from benevolent intent, Vallée is content to accept their lead in matters of culture and spirituality. Simply by functioning in a way that cannot be explained by scientific means, the UFOs have convinced him

194

that they must be trusted; at no point does he question whether their intention is to harm us.

Although Vallée has appeared to enjoy his status as being the dissenting voice amongst UFO researchers, there are signs that his multi-dimensional theories are gaining support. On 15th March 2015, Express (the online version of the U.K. newspaper The Daily Express) published an article focussed on a video that had captured glowing objects appearing and disappearing in the skies over Canada. Although the footage was criticised by some researchers, others such as the The Cryptid Research Group recognised it as evidence of UFOs travelling between dimensions. On 14th May 2018 *Live Science* published a paper titled "Aliens May Well Exist in a Parallel Universe, New Studies Find"(15) in which Brandon Spektor quoted studies in the journal Monthly Notices of the Royal Astronomical Society which proposed that life could exist on planets in other universes. The article refers to the multiverse theory which argues that there may be an infinite number of universes, an old philosophical response to the question of why this universe has just the right strengths of forces to sustain life: the answer being that amongst an infinite number there was bound to exist one like ours. It has been a long-held belief amongst atheists denying a Creator, but as a philosophical argument is weak, since it demands an infinite number of universes to counter faith in One God. But the article turns to the mysteries of so-called dark energy (something that current thinking suggests makes up seventy percent of our universe) of which we know very little (or even if it actually exists). The article quotes the work of Pascal Elahi who claims that his experiments demonstrate that the existence of life is highly probable in universes with very different levels of dark energy, and that physicists should be prepared to embrace new theories of existence in order to accommodate the latest scientific discoveries. The familiar theme of change and abandonment of old ideas is clearly at the fore. Even amongst the serious scientific journals, the multi-dimensions hypothesis is being accepted.

Discover published an article titled "Three Totally Mind-bending Implications of a Multidimensional Universe"(16) in which David Warmflash points to Edwin Hubble's discovery of a growing universe as evidence of dimensions beyond those which we can perceive. Warmflash argues that the implications include the possibility of warp-drive, he suggests that advanced civilisations might be able to manipulate other dimensions in order to travel between galaxies. Time travel is also a realistic possibility according to Warmflash, and of course, multi-dimensions raises the possibility of worm holes – an idea pursued by Carl Sagan, which suggests that tunnels linking different areas of time-space might be the means by which visitors are able to reach our planet. Amongst all these theories there is a repeated reference to the hospitable planets that inevitably exist, and are simply waiting for our arrival.

Before we begin to accept the multi-universe theory, it should be noted that there are many scientific and philosophical objections. By definition, if something exists outside our universe, it can never be proven by anything contained within it. John Horgan expounds this point in the article "Multiverse Theories Are Bad for Science" published by *Scientific American*.(17) In another article titled "Is speculation in multiverses as immoral as speculation in subprime mortgages?" Horgan decries the pointlessness of multi-dimensional theories, he criticises "the descent of theoretical physics into increasingly fantastical speculation, disconnected from the reality that we can access empirically."(18) Horgan reminds us that "Multiverse theories aren't theories—they're science fictions, theologies, works of the imagination unconstrained by evidence."(19)

While a pursuit of theoretical physics may not be as morally dubious as Horgan suggests, it is true that the concept has appealed to those with an inclination to investigate more occult topics. One of the most important characters in the contemporary field of UFO research is Dr Steven Greer, and as we shall see, his promotion of esoteric themes alongside belief in UFOs is closely linked with the idea of multi-dimensions.

Endnotes

1 – Good, Timothy, *Above Top Secret*, p.185
2 – ibid. Good, pp.313-314
3 – ibid. Good, p.133
4 – ibid. Good, p.435
5 – ibid. Good, p.328
6 – Good, Timothy, *Alien Base, The Evidence For Extraterrestrial Colonisation Of Earth*, Arrow Books 1999, p.59
7 – Steiger, Brad, *Project Blue Book: The Top Secret UFO Findings Revealed!* Ballantine Books 1976
8 – Vallée, Jacques, *Dimensions,* p.146
9 – ibid. Vallée, p.146
10 – Dr Michio Taku and Jennifer Trainer argue this in their book *Beyond Einstein*
11 – A claim made by the French physicist Costa de Beauregard
12 – op cit. Vallée, *Dimensions*, p.148
13 - ibid. Vallée, p.149
14 – ibid. Vallée, p.149
15 – The full article may be found here: https://www.livescience.com/62558-parallel-universe-aliens-survive-dark-energy.html
16 – The full article may be found here: https://www.discovermagazine.com/the-sciences/three-totally-mind-bending-implications-of-a-multidimensional-universe
17 – The full article can be found here: https://blogs.scientificamerican.com/cross-check/multiverse-theories-are-bad-for-science/

18 – The full article may be found here: https://blogs.scientificamerican.com/cross-check/is-speculation-in-multiverses-as-immoral-as-speculation-in-subprime-mortgages/
19 – ibid. Horgan, John

Chapter Thirteen – Steven Greer and Disclosure

One of the most predominant themes found on UFO websites, chatrooms and in published works, is the idea that governments (though usually the U.S. government) are preparing public consciousness for the revelation of the existence of extraterrestrials. Rumours of proposed dates come and go, much like Seventh Day Adventist warnings about the end of the world, and each time the event fails to materialise, a new date replaces the previous one. The desire for disclosure (as believers call it) is so intense that the disappointment of previous promises quickly fades and is replaced with expectation for the next. The issue is not as simple as one might assume since there is enough evidence to suggest that official bodies are contributing to these expectations, though for different reasons than UFO researchers might believe. There are also a number of key figures promoting hope of disclosure, chief among them being Steven M. Greer, M.D. who we will examine in detail.

As long ago as 1975 there were supposed leaks from military and government officials that disclosure was coming soon. Timothy Good states that U.S. Senator Barry Goldwater, who served as

Chairman of the Senate Intelligence Committee, was refused permission to look at many documents about UFOs, and in a letter stated that with regards to files concerning supposed alien bodies kept at Langley, Virginia:

It is still classified as Top Secret. There is a plan under way to release some, if not all of this material in the near future. I'm just as anxious to see the material as you are.(1)

The allure of the "near future" is a sufficiently attractive carrot dangling before those who want to believe in aliens that in almost no researcher's material do we find retrospective questions being asked about such claims. The reason for this goes beyond the individual psychology of the researcher. To be seen as a doubter or even one who asks difficult questions can quickly cut researchers off from their audience, and in some cases, deny them access to the financial revenue that sustaining belief can bring. Those who contribute to the sense of expectation are simply giving their audience what they want.

Steven Greer began his research into UFOs in 1993, when, as he says, he wanted to:

identify first hand military and government witnesses to UFO events and projects, as well as other evidence to be used in a public disclosure.(2)

His intention from the very beginning was to add to the pressure on governments to reveal what he believed was the secret evidence about aliens and their technology. Greer claims that from the very beginning of his work he was advising the Clinton administration about UFOs,(3) and it is this link with government officials that he has always used as a means of claiming credibility for his statements. Of course, Greer does not question to what extent he himself may be being used as a means of spreading disinformation by government. A key reason Greer believes he is the one unearthing truth, rather than serving as a mouthpiece for some agency's psychological operation, is the occasions he requested Congressional hearings but was refused. He is so convinced in the importance of his discoveries that such denials become for him unquestionable evidence for a cover up, rather than indications that government officials may not be taking him as seriously as he believes.

In response to these frustrations, Greer set out to create the *Witness Archive Project*, which has grown to over a hundred hours of video interviews with ex-military personnel describing their accounts of UFO encounters. The interviews had been collected by December 2000, and Greer edited them himself. He has since claimed that it was the intense work schedule he was under, his lack of editing experience and the severe shortage of funds, that account for the number of errors in names which appear in the documents he produced. What Greer ended up with was around a hundred people who made quite bizarre and sometimes outrageous claims.

Since revealing his evidence to the world, Greer has gone on to make a number of public appearances and now has a Netflix movie called *Unacknowledged*. His focus of complaint is now not just that governments are suppressing the existence of aliens, but that they are also keeping advanced technology for themselves; such as something he calls zero-point or quantum vacuum energy which he says could solve the world's environmental problems by providing pollution free energy and also end world hunger. Many vague and unsubstantiated claims are made throughout the film *Unacknowledged*, and it even includes an appearance by Richard C. Doty who has admitted feeding UFO researchers with false information, but Greer presents him as a direct witness to aliens who crashed in Roswell.(4) Another example showing how Greer trusts his witnesses because of their military background is Major George A. Filer, who appears in Greer's movie claiming to have chased a UFO over Stonehenge. Even a brief examination of Filer's past reveals that he has previously claimed that Mars was inhabited by aliens who blew themselves up in a nuclear war, and that the evidence for their civilisation can still be seen all over Mars.(5)

One final example of the questionable credibility of Greer's witnesses is Sergeant Karl Wolfe. In the movie, and famously in the famous National Press Club in Washington DC in 2001, Wolfe claimed to have seen photographs of alien structures on the dark side of the moon in 1965, taken by the Lunar

Orbiter, while he was working at the headquarters of Tactical Air Command in Langley. A fellow worker there, he says, secretly showed him the photographs and said they had found an alien base there. Though it makes for an entertaining story, the reality is that The Lunar Orbiter Program didn't begin until 1966 and the first photographs of the dark side of the moon weren't taken until the Lunar Orbiter 4 mission in May 1967. Such factual errors would be enough for most people, but for believers in aliens the response is simply to claim that the real mission happened earlier, and that it is a further example of government secrecy and suppression of truth. Sadly, there is plenty of evidence to prove that governments of all political persuasion lie to their people, but the enormous cost of the lunar missions was such that in order to maintain public support for the expenditure, NASA was desperate to present photographs at the earliest possibility. It would have been much easier just to conceal the necessary photographs from all those taken rather than cover up the entire mission. Similarly, there is far greater risk of being found out hiding the launch, flight and return of the Lunar Orbiter than removing a few photographs from the file that gets shown to the press. NASA has published 419 high resolution photographs from the mission (as well as 127 medium resolution shots), none of them reveal alien bases.

It isn't simply an unquestioning willingness to believe in witnesses because of their military background that undermines Greer's arguments.

There is a clear case of him choosing to misrepresent the truth in order to support his case. In Unacknowledged, Buzz Aldrin is presented as claiming to believe in an alien object on one of Mars' moons, Phobos. In the film he is shown saying:

There's a monolith, a very unusual structure
on this little potato-shaped object that goes
around Mars once in every seven hours.
They're going to say, "Who put that there?
Who put that there?

This version of the question clearly implies that it was aliens who put it there. However, Greer has misled his audience. In the full, unedited statement, Aldrin is saying something not only different, but is in fact making the exact opposite point. He said:

There's a monolith, a very unusual structure
on this little potato-shaped object that goes
around Mars once in every seven hours.
They're going to say, "Who put that there?
Who put that there?" Well, the universe put
it there. If you choose, God put it there.(6)

If Greer truly believed in the reality of aliens, and the reliability of his witnesses, we might ask why he would manipulate a statement this way. Further, anyone familiar with *2001: A Space Odyssey* will immediately think of the smooth, crafted monoliths left by the fictional visitors of the movie, but in reality the object on Phobos is an irregular, clearly natural phenomenon, a piece of rock jutting out from the moon.

One of Greer's techniques in his talks is to refer to multiple government officials who have given him secret briefings, but to never provide hard evidence. The same pattern occurs in *Unacknowledged*. The only evidence ever provided is the claims of the witnesses themselves, and when we begin to see that some of their testimony is flawed, the whole case falls apart. As we have seen, Carl Sagan completely rejected the possibility of alien technology being advanced enough to carry them here, but Greer makes the claim that Sagan was a believer who had been silenced by government agencies. This contradicts multiple statements across a large body of Sagan's work, and reveals Greer to once more be deliberately misleading his audience. Greer also uses quotations from Sagan in the *Disclosure Briefing Document*, perhaps in the hope of claiming some of the astronomer's credibility for his own work, despite the irony of using a writer who rejected the very premise Greer is forwarding.(7)

Greer's philosophy has become mixed with many occult and esoteric ideas, but at the heart of his teaching is a utopian materialism. It is the belief in the potential for the creation of a society where peace reigns, and humanity is free to explore the cosmos. He says that government agencies:

possess fully operational anti-gravity propulsion
devices and new energy generation systems
that, if declassified and put to peaceful uses,
would empower a new human civilization
without want, poverty or environmental

damage.(8)

These kinds of promises have been made by many different political and social groups. Whether it is through communism, capitalism, or secret alien technology, people's longing for an end to world problems, whether real or invented, can lead them to accept extreme ideas. These fantasies almost always lead to the intense suffering of certain groups of people. Utopia on earth is a demonic lie, freedom from suffering will only be found in the Kingdom of Heaven. Greer's response to such charges is "This is not a fantasy or a hoax. Do not believe those who say that this is not possible: they are the intellectual descendants of those who said the Wright brothers would never fly."(9) One of the warning signs of any philosophy is when it calls on the overthrow of old institutions and ways of life. Greer espouses radical change to our lives, he says:

it is obvious that these technologies that
are currently classified would enable
human civilization to achieve sustainability.
Of course, in the near term, we are talking
about the greatest social, economic
and technological revolution in human history
- bar none.(10)

Once more we witness belief in UFOs as a part of an old revolutionary spirit, fulfilling a passion for rebellion and change. Greer predicts that unless such transformation comes about, there will be what he calls worldwide geopolitical and social collapse. No longer just a carrot, but now a stick too.

Greer has claimed that since he was a child he has been able to make contact with extraterrestrials by entering states of meditation. He has developed these techniques and has led hundreds of what he calls "vectoring" sessions. Participants pay for the experience of being taken by Greer to encounter "aliens". Before being allowed to accompany him they are required to sign a non-disclosure agreement, and so the only accounts of these sessions come from Greer himself. For a man who has spent so much time criticising secretive government agencies for not releasing the evidence about UFOs, one might assume Greer would have released an extensive catalogue of videos showing the encounters up close. In fact, other than a few Youtube videos containing nothing more than unidentifiable lights so far away they could be anything, Greer has produced no credible evidence of any kind. The clips show numbers of cameras and recording equipment, but all they capture is Greer telling those present that the light behind the trees has come from another dimension. One wonders why, when he makes the claim(11) that he has made contact with extraterrestrials at close range (as he describes it), he hasn't disclosed the evidence to the world. Greer deflects such questions by claiming that the advanced technology of the visitors is such that it cannot be captured on conventional recording equipment, and that the real encounter is within.

His claim now is that only through the attainment of what he calls "higher states of consciousness" through meditation, can human beings contact extraterrestrials.(12) This higher state permits levitation, telekinesis, celestial vision, the capacity to heal and teleportation (he claims all of this in *Collection of Position Papers by Dr. Steven Greer on Cosmology and Contact*). In his series of You Tube Videos titled CE-5 (after his latest film Close Encounters of the Fifth Kind) he promotes mediation and a CE-5 app that encourages people to form teams and practise his techniques. Greer promotes this philosophy as "the science of consciousness" which has as its goal the "oneness" of humanity and the raising of human consciousness. For anyone familiar with world religions, none of this terminology will be new. Greer acknowledges that he is a student of what he calls "Sanskrit Vedas"; we should note that Sanskrit is simply the language they are written in, the Vedas are Hindu. But Greer is selecting which Hindu practices and beliefs suit his worldview, he rejects any supernatural explanation of extraterrestrials.(13) However, he declares himself a pantheist when he states that not only is the universe full of life, but that the universe is alive and intelligent. This intelligence, he proposes, is not a spiritual entity, but nature's eternal mind.(14) Greer does make statements that conform to the truth of Orthodoxy. He recognises that extraterrestrials are non-biological beings who possess intelligence and can interact with us.(15) As we shall see, this fits perfectly with the teachings of the Church Fathers, but his conclusion about their origin, purpose and intentions are dangerously wrong. He now has access to millions of people through his programmes on CBS, the BBC, The Discovery Channel, the History Channel, Netflix and others. Audiences who have no understanding of the traditions of the Church are being exposed to his philosophy. Greer claims that his "new cosmology" adds to our understanding of God, but simply because he uses the same word, we must not imagine he is talking about the same God. Greer recognises that there are non-physical "spiritual" beings at work in the universe, what he calls "Astral Beings",(16) and argues that they have been misunderstood to be angels or demons, and even aliens too. This is why he thinks UFO researchers have struggled to explain the phenomenon, because their cosmology doesn't include both the biological and non-biological beings that are visiting us. While wanting to insist that aliens are real, he has had to acknowledge that in many cases, the alien story does not explain the event. But instead of questioning whether UFOs really do come from other planets, he has created a cosmology to incorporate multiple types of beings.

On 10th April 2021 Greer warned of an impending change in the U.S. government's stance on UFOs, claiming that aliens will be declared a global threat to humanity, and that this will enable even greater secrecy to be imposed. However, this he warns, is leading to a hoax alien event which will use "Project Bluebeam" as a means of creating holographic images to mislead us. While it is possible that governments could use such technology in this way, we must remember that the success of such a hoax is dependent on public belief in UFOs, belief that he has been instrumental in fostering.(17)

Of course it is not only Greer who promotes the belief in an impending disclosure. In his book *Dimensions*, Jacques Vallee describes how he came to believe that the film *Close Encounters of the Third Kind* had been supported by government agencies with the intention of preparing people for the release of UFO information. As part of a series of broadcasts and documentaries, he believes the movie was intended to both guide public opinion, but also to gauge reaction. Since more than forty-five years has now passed since the film's release, it now looks like a typical element in the generation of expectation that actually results in nothing.

Even as I write this in 2021, UFO researchers have a new date to anticipate when government documents are going to be released. No doubt more pilot-recorded clips will emerge, and more images of vague, unidentifiable shapes will be heralded as fresh evidence for UFOs being alien craft. Human psychology has been manipulated in this way for a long time, and so long as the desire for the story to be true remains, it seems the promoters of the myth will continue to be excused of their failure to ever deliver on their promise of disclosure.

Endnotes

1 – From a letter written by Senator Goldwater, quoted by Timothy Good in *Above Top Secret* p.400

2 – Greer, Steven, *Executive Summary of the Disclosure Project Briefing Document* 2001 p.4

3 – ibid. Greer, Steven, p.4

4 - 2. Hayakawa, Norio. *Did Richard C. Doty ruin the life of Albuquerque businessman,* Paul Bennewitz? Found at http://bit.ly/2CCWirH

5 – Robert Schaeffer described Filer making these claims at a MUFON (Mutual UFO Network) symposium in 2011

6 – Aldrin, Buzz, making the statement here http://bit.ly/2CPHcwx

7 – op.cit Greer, Steven, Executive Summary of the *Disclosure Project Briefing Document* p.6

8 – ibid. Greer, Steven, p.7

9 – ibid. Greer, Steven p.9

10 – ibid. Greer, Steven, p.9

11 – Greer makes this claim on p.3 of an online document titled Collection of Position Papers by Dr. Steven Greer on Cosmology and Contact

12 – Greer promotes this teaching in his book Contact: Countdown To Transformation

13 – Greer rejects supernatural interpretations of alien encounters as being a consequence of human ignorance on p.8 of Collection of Position Papers by Dr. Steven Greer on Cosmology and Contact

14 – ibid. Greer, Steven, p.10

15 – ibid. Greer, Steven, p.11

16 –ibid. Greer, Steven, p.16

17 – Greer's 10/04/21 statement can be located at https:goldenageofgaia/2021/04/10/urgent-breaking-news-update-from-dr-steven-greer/

Chapter Fourteen – Carl Gustav Jung

Modern UFO researchers, on the whole, treat the phenomenon as an objective experience which can be studied and analysed like any other event. Though many are now recognising the psychic and religious dimensions, their efforts are founded on the belief that something is happening that will take place whether it is observed or not; in other words it is not dependent on or taking place for the observer. This is a serious error.

In 1959 the Swiss psychologist Carl Jung published a theory that the phenomenon can only be understood in terms of its psychological and religious meaning.(1) In 1957 he was asked to investigate and share his ideas of how a shared fear of nuclear annihilation was linked to the growing number of UFO sightings. Jung applied many of his familiar theories to UFOs; such as that they fit his understanding of archetypes, that they appear in dreams and that they may be a psychic projection of the collective unconscious. However, he had to acknowledge that none of this could account for the physical impact that UFO encounters can have, or that they are frequently detected by radar. Jung called UFOs "technological angels", and though he was adapting what he considered a myth to fit his own psychological paradigm, as we shall see, his terminology was closer to the reality than he realised.

Jung served as a consultant to the *Aerial Phenomena Research Organisation* (APRO) but stated that he had been interested in UFOs since 1946. He found too many aspects of the phenomenon did not fit entirely into any psychological explanation, and while sceptics have quoted details from his work to demonstrate his rejection of any objective reality, one of his conclusions that is rarely reproduced was that:

A purely psychological explanation is ruled out by the fact that a large number of observations indicate a natural one, even a physical one...The American Air Force (despite its contradictory statements) as well as the Canadian, consider the observations to be real....However, the discs do not behave in accordance with physical laws but as though without weight, and they show signs of intelligent guidance.(2)

Jung was convinced that governments were deliberately misleading the public on the matter, and though he often spoke out in frustration over this, he was willing to accept the extraterrestrial explanation as a possible motive for their approach. He wrote:

If the extraterrestrial origin of the phenomena should be confirmed, it would put us, without doubt, in the extremely

precarious position of primitive communities
today in conflict with the superior culture of
the whites; the rudder would be removed
from our grasp, and we should lose our
pleasant dreams.(3)

Despite such bold statements Jung was wary of committing himself entirely to a non-psychological explanation. In his book *Flying Saucers: A Modern Myth of Things Seen in the Skies*, he states that those believing themselves to have seen a UFO were really victims of what he labelled "projection creating fantasy": he argued that the feeling of potential global destruction from nuclear war was provoking people to imagine that the fate of human kind was in the hands of semi-gods who could intervene to save us. Jung may have had a personal interest in the nature of UFOs, but his writing focusses on asking why so many people were claiming to see them and how the phenomenon can be linked to an existential threat. He created the now familiar term "modern myth" to account for this process, arguing that UFOs were simply an "external event" that mirrors the "internal psychic" state. Jung dismissed the religious experiences of people in the past and claimed that UFOs were merely the modern version of what he termed "psychic fantasies"; the longing for saving intervention from outside forces. Once again, he is closer to the Orthodox understanding than he would have realised, and the loss of Christian belief is a factor we shall explore further when reflecting on the writings of the Church Fathers.

Such is the nature of UFOs that when a famous psychologist writes about them there is inevitably going to be a lot of public and media interest. It is interesting to note that press coverage at the time swung back and forth in its claims that Jung was either endorsing or denying the reality of their existence. It began in 1954 when he was approached by the Swiss newspaper *Die Weltwoche* for an interview on the topic. He responded with two letters which were printed in full, as long articles in July 1954. It was here that he acknowledged having been studying the phenomenon for eight years, and concluded that though something was being seen, he was unable to say what it was. It was in these letters that he stated that he believed the U.S. Air Force was creating panic amongst the public with what he considered dishonest statements. In fact, his own inability to fully explain the phenomenon, and the Air Force's confusing public position, are both a consequence of the incompatibility of secular assumptions with the nature of the events. We may go as far to say that the same problem exists for many victims of these UFO encounters who struggle to find a logical explanation for what can be bizarre experiences. It makes no sense, for example, for Jung to try to argue that something which abducts or physically interacts with a person can be a projection of our collective unconscious. Jung's recognition of how many in the West have turned away from traditional religious belief leads him to falsely imagine that a religious, myth-making function of the psyche has simply replaced the God of Christianity with a non-paranormal myth of aliens and spaceships. But this only creates further difficulties in his thinking, when he presents modern man as a rational, atheistic creature who is burdened with a religious longing at his core. Jung concluded that a conflict exists within those who have consciously chosen to reject the existence of God because the collective unconscious compensates for this conscious choice by creating hallucinations of UFOs to replace God: it is, he believed, nothing more than a primitive urge to look up. As we shall see, the religious nature of many UFO encounters, such a witnesses being given prophetic messages for mankind, do match some patterns of religious experience, but again, this is not by chance.

Jung was deeply interested in mandalas, which he believed were a graphical representation of the self. The word comes from the Hindi for circle or centre. They can be found in many religious and occult traditions, such as Buddhism, astrology, and Hinduism. For example, a mandala can be used in yoga when those meditating attempt to internalise the image and so, practitioners believe, its energy too. For Jung, there was an obvious connection between these geometric shapes and UFOs, Jung believed that in our dreams the mandala symbolises the process of centering the ego in relation to a person's psychic wholeness. Jung encouraged his clients to spontaneously draw mandalas as part of their therapy and Jung practised the technique himself. He learned how to do this while staying at a Buddhist monastery in Darjeeling, and explained that the mandala is "an inner image which is built up through active imagination".(4) It is revealing that while Jung rejected traditional Christian belief, he accepted the teachings of eastern religions. He saw in their teachings something he could match with his own psychological theories, he said:

It seems to me beyond question that these
Eastern symbols originated in dreams
and visions, and were not invented by
some Mahayana church father.(5)

The attraction of mandalas was the belief that they somehow represented the centre of the true self which was not affected by the ego. Jung was happy to confer on them what he considered a "metaphysical nature".(6)

For Jung the circle is an archetype of a whole, united self. For this reason he believed that in times of crisis (such as a potential nuclear war) the mind will produce visions of this shape in its attempt to overcome threat or disorganisation. There are many modern forms of creative art therapies that now use mandalas as part of their process. It is not difficult to see how images of UFOs would fit into this.

Jung's attitude to religious belief is confused. He described having meaningful visions and dreams as a child, but the anti-climax of his first communion (non-Orthodox) left him with the conviction that human beings crave something beyond faith. Jung went on to interpret all theological concepts as being manifestations of man's psychology, even

219

reducing the Holy Trinity to aspects of the self. He was far more open to the influences of eastern beliefs, even contributing to books on yoga, the I Ching, and *The Tibetan Book of the Dead*. He was drawn to the teachings of Gnosticism where he saw many parallels between his own theories and gnostic mythology.(7) Later in life he wore jewellery engraved with gnostic symbols. He went on to compose his own "gnostic hymn", called *The Seven Sermons of the Dead*, which he refused to allow to be published under his real name while he was alive. He claimed that the book was dictated to him by a spirit guide from another dimension. Once more we see here how Jung's public, professional writings were potentially at odds with his own personal beliefs.

Jung's interest in UFOs sits alongside his fascination with a number of occult and paranormal phenomena, an interest which grew after he had a near-death experience. He grew up in a household where his mother practised mediumship and spoke in tongues, and his grandfather learned Hebrew because he believed that this was the language spoken in Heaven. Perhaps not surprisingly, coming from such an intensely charged environment, Jung wrote a number of scientific treatises on astrology, spiritualism and parapsychology. He gave lectures insisting that scientists recognise the limits of their research and knowledge, and when Freud advised him to guard his interest from the public for fear of destroying his reputation, he responded with a letter in which he said:

There are strange and wondrous things in these lands of darkness. Please don't worry about my wanderings in these infinitudes. I shall return laden with rich booty for our knowledge of the human psyche. For a while longer I must intoxicate myself on magic perfumes in order to fathom the secrets that lie hidden in the abyss of the unconscious.(8)

Jung's interest led him to participate in séances (he first attended at the age of nineteen) and made a study of ten mediums. He was convinced that some mediums possessed the ability to levitate and was critical of anyone who denied his claims. He believed that medicine-men from other cultures could contact the spirits of the dead and criticised western science for failing to confirm the reality of telepathic communication. Jung was typical of the age, many other prominent scientists were involved in occult research. For example, the physicist John Strutt who received the Nobel Prize in 1964, Hans Driesch who was the first biologist to perform animal cloning, Ian Stevenson, the head of the psychiatry department at the University of Virginia, all served as president of the Society for Psychical Research (which has as its stated aim, the investigation of all that is psychic and paranormal). For Jung the interest extended to believing that his daughter was a clairvoyant who could communicate with his grandmother and in 1916 he

221

founded the Psychology Club which was devoted to studying spiritual topics. In his book *The Aryan Christ: The Secret Life of Carl Jung*, Richard Noll claims that Jung had a particular hatred of Orthodox Christianity which he made efforts to attack in the hope of spreading belief in polytheism. By the end of the 1920s he had become obsessed with Zoroastrianism and alchemy, still maintaining that the West was suffering as a result of the Christian influence on its morality. Although he married in 1902, desiring to reject this Christian influence, he embraced a pagan notion of polygamy and began sexual relationships with two of his patients, Sabina Spilrein and Toni Wolff.

Before he died, Jung admitted that his theories and investigations had brought him no closer to understanding the true nature of existence. He described himself as a "stranger to his own amassed knowledge". He was able to acknowledge the huge contradictions in his ideas, and that he would die with only as much wisdom as had been born with. This is important for us to remember when we survey the many works on UFOs that claim him as an authoritive figure who gives legitimacy to their various beliefs. Once more we see the connection between interest in UFOs and other occult phenomena, and it is clear that for the Orthodox Christian, Jungian psychology is spiritually dangerous. We will now develop this theme, and consider the link more widely between UFOs and religious beliefs.

Endnotes

1 - Jung, Carl Gustav, *Flying Saucers: A Modern Myth of Things Seen in the Skies* (translated by R.F. Hull) Routledge and Kegan Paul), London 1959

2 – Jung, Carl Gustav, "Unidentified Flying Objects", FSR Vol.1 No.2 1955 p.p.17-18 (originally appearing in *Courier Interplanetaire*, Switzerland 1954)

3 – ibid. Jung, p.p.17-18

4 – Jung, Carl, *Psychology and Alchemy*, Princeton University Press, 1993, paragraph 123

5 - ibid. Jung, paragraph 124

6 – ibid. Jung, paragraph 126

7 – Jung was particularly interested in the Apocryphon of John

8 – In a letter Jung wrote to Freud, dated 8th May, 1911

Chapter Fifteen – Occultism, The Vatican and Alien Saviours

We have seen how so many of those attracted to the topic of UFOs are also drawn to other occult areas. In fact the link with many dangerous and heretical religious ideas quickly becomes evident as one reads the texts produced by UFO researchers. In the absence of a verifiable explanation, many have turned to more esoteric answers, often drawing on different traditions and teachings to create a system of belief that satisfies them. We will now look more closely at these links, as well as how the Vatican has embraced the possibility of UFOs, and how there is a growing expectation amongst UFO believers that extraterrestrials may offer a form of salvation, even if it is a materialistic one.

Researcher John Kiel began studying UFOs in 1945 and claimed to have received many letters from people who had encountered them. His conclusions were clear, he wrote:

To deal with UFOs is just as dangerous as black magic. Nervous, gullible, and inexperienced people, as a rule, become a victim of the phenomenon. In many cases

*this leads to acute schizophrenia, demon
mania, even suicide. Thus the mysterious
charm of the UFO phenomenon can lead
to terrible tragedies. Therefore I
strongly recommend parents: forbid children
to pursue an interest in such issues. It is the
duty of teachers and of any adult person
to protect children from UFO hobbies.*(1)

In Chapter seventeen we will examine the teachings of the Church Fathers that demonstrate that the idea that UFOs are of alien origin is a disguise, as Kiel describes it, a Trojan horse within which great evil is concealed. Kiel argues that there is evidence of UFO presence often when human blood is being shed on the battlefield, and that though they communicate promises of scientific advancement, they invariably bring or appear at times of suffering.

The respected UFO researcher J. Allen Hynek concluded that in order to account for the various aspects of UFO sightings and the effects they have on people, it is necessary to investigate their psychic nature. This is an idea supported throughout the writings of Vallée. As early as the 1950s there were many researchers coming to the same conclusion, but the prevailing attitudes of the day meant this opinion was rejected as resembling the teachings of a cult, and the extraterrestrial hypothesis seemed more scientific and rational. Hynek is far from alone in reaching this conclusion. Brad Steiger, a professor from Iowa, was given the opportunity to read the Operation

Blue Book files in 1977. He determined that UFOs are a multi-dimensional paraphysical phenomenon,(2) and produced a number of widely read books explaining how UFOs fit into the broader world of paranormal phenomena.

Though writers like Steiger always focussed on these kinds of topics, other UFO researchers have begun with more conventional ideas and have been slowly drawn into occult realms. The best example of this is Timothy Good. His early research was motivated by his interest in aviation, and his first works communicate the sense of someone who is simply analysing the evidence. However, as his research continued there is a notable shift in his writing and he was clearly affected by the occult nature of UFOs. Writing about yogi teachers in 1998 he states:

> ...highly advanced avatars and masters said to
> be living on Earth who can levitate, render
> themselves invisible, project their image
> across vast distances, walk through walls etc.
> But this in no way alters the fact that
> these remarkable people are still flesh and
> blood human beings, albeit highly
> advanced physically, mentally and spiritually.
> It is my conviction that many extra-terrestrials,
> too, are capable of these and other fantastic
> feats: indeed, in this respect I see little
> difference between highly evolved human
> beings said to live on this planet and those
> from any other.(3)

Good goes on to describe attending spiritualist séances in London(4) and presents the claim that most people who encounter what they believe to be aliens only suffer depression because they feel a futility at trying to convince others of their experience.(5) This openness to the esoteric nature of UFOs inevitably leads to a rejection of traditional Christianity. Good relates how the aliens promise to reveal themselves on a large scale once humanity has accepted their spiritual teachings. He repeats the message given to a man in New Mexico named Aolinar Alberto Villa, which claimed:

When the law of love rules the minds of the men of Earth, then the people of other worlds will come in great numbers and share with us their advanced ideas.(6)

In a section of his book titled Servant Of God, Good describes an encounter relayed to him by what he called a contactee from India. During the encounter the man met what he and Good believed to be an alien called Satu, and the contactee told Good:

Satu pointed to an image of Lord Vishnu, one of the principle deities, with images of strange aerial craft painted on to the sacred cloth. "This is proof that earlier generations have observed the effigy of our out-of-space crafts having made an earlier landing," said Satu.(7)

Later Good quotes the alleged alien, Satu, as teaching "Religion is blind, just like love".(8) This is the new age philosophy that Father Seraphim Rose warned about in *Orthodoxy and the Religion*

227

of the Future, a faith without doctrinal boundaries that declares all belief as equal and equally valid. This illusion of harmony is reinforced when Good relates the journey to an alien planet where "Everybody looked happy in this utopian society". The fantasy of a materialistic utopia has been the promise of a number of political regimes that have brought unimaginable suffering to humanity; particularly to Christians. The New Age philosophy of the aliens described in Good's later books becomes a full-blown pantheism when an extraterrestrial declares "their people make no distinction between God and nature...because God is nature and nature is God."(9)

The attempt to create a materialistic explanation for UFOs quickly fails when faced with the non-materialistic aspects, but having committed to an idea of aliens, then it becomes necessary to attribute advanced spiritual capabilities to them. UFO believers then become even more vulnerable to the experience because they accept the spiritual messages, regardless of their content. The theory of evolution helps support this position, since what is taken as superior technology is also seen as evidence of a more advanced species. Timothy Good relates such an idea in one of his later books, he writes:

There are so many theories – this thing is so complex. One theory is that the Earth is the only one in the solar system which was given the gift of life, and this life developed a long time ago on this planet, and reached

*a civilisation far beyond ours, in technology
and spiritual ideas, thousands, maybe millions
of years ago.*(10)

Even for those who do not form such theories on
the basis of their experience, UFO encounters can
deeply change someone's religious outlook. As one
witness described to Good:

*The experience changed my character greatly
and had a profound effect on my attitude to all
questions of religion and politics. It was
the greatest experience of my life.*(11)

It is worth noting that almost all UFO researchers
and witnesses, when talking about the impact of the
UFO experience on religious belief, treat faith from
a non-Orthodox perspective. They talk about ideas
and theories, as though Christian faith was no more
than a collection of rational constructs that can be
examined and changed like those on any other
topic. But the tendency to embrace more new age
attitudes is also very common, and suggests a
reluctance to accept the teachings of traditional
faith. For example, Eugene Cernam, a member of
the Apollo 17 mission, stated in a documentary
filmed in 2007 that the experience of being in space
had convinced him that "There has to be somebody
bigger then you, and bigger than me, and I mean
this in a spiritual sense, not a religious sense."

UFOs have not only influenced religious beliefs,
they have been central to the creation of new
religions, such as the Raelians and Heaven's Gate.
Marshall Applewhite, the leader of the Heaven's
Gate Sect, convinced thirty-nine cult members to

join him in committing mass suicide at a Santa Fe ranch in the belief that their souls would be picked up by a passing spaceship that was hiding behind the Hale-Bopp comet. But even more mainstream faiths have adapted to accommodate UFOs, such both the Nation of Islam, and Sikhism, which now teach that God did not place life on Earth alone, but spread it throughout the universe. Often religious groups who form around the image of the grey alien have no formal doctrines or practices, which can be part of their attraction since they make no demands on a follower's way of life or ethical choices. Supernatural ideas are such that they can be adapted to fit any context or narrative, even the modern technological era. There is a good deal of research into parapsychology that is leading to recognition of a greater connection between some fields of science and the occult. There are even a number of Protestant and Roman Catholic "theologians" now claiming that God's infinite mystery must surely require an array of intelligent life forms in order for His glory to be manifested. Such a statement fails to grasp the distinction between infinity and any number, whether it be one or tens of millions: God's glory cannot be manifested fully in millions of life forms any more than one since He is without limit.

Religious traditions rely on testimonials and personal accounts to share the experience at the heart of their beliefs. The witness accounts of the Apostles and the countless saints through Church history have been the basis for much of Orthodox tradition. Therefore, UFO researchers who also depend on the accounts of witnesses may claim that their teachings are equally valid. However, the testimonials of those who have been transformed in positive ways, sometimes miraculously, are completely different to the stories of those who have been left confused, depressed, afraid and sometimes suicidal. If, as we will show in chapter seventeen, the UFO experience is the action of demons, then the messages and understanding of those who have been affected by them must be rejected. Certainly Dr Vallée's conclusions support this, he writes "Human beings are under the control of a strange force that bends them in absurd ways, forcing them to play a role in a bizarre game of deception."(12) Deception is a common theme amongst the accounts of many contactees, who often feel that they have been mocked by the treatment of the aliens. For Vallée, this is nothing more than a "control system", and he believes that the purpose of this is to manipulate human beliefs. A number of contactees have described how they have felt the urge to make telepathic communication with the extraterrestrials, almost feeling as though they were praying to them in order to make contact.

The first Dutchman to go to space was Wubbo Ockels. Before his death he wrote an open letter to world authorities that can be viewed online. Amongst his calls for green technology he says:

With a new belief in humanity we can create a new religion that brings us all together….

*There are many religions that get people
together, but never all people. The different
gods in whom they believe
separate humanity…these religions do not
unify humanity with the earth. They
are not sustainable…we cannot hide behind
God because it is us.*(13)

Such a statement hardly needs comment, and of course, its message was universally embraced in the mainstream media and by various environmental and new age groups. It indicates a growing attitude amongst many scientists that sees Christianity as a restrictive influence, while other beliefs offer opportunities because they may be incorporated into the latest scientific theories.

With governments "leaking" just enough information to keep people intrigued while failing to answer any substantive questions, the official response only perpetuates what is happening, as Vallée describes it:

*If you wanted to bypass the intelligentsia and
the church, remain undetectable to the military
system, leave undisturbed the political
and administrative levels of a society, and at
the same time implant deep within that
society far-reaching doubts concerning its
basic philosophical tenets, this is exactly how
you would have to act. At the same time
of course, such a process would have to
provide its own explanation to make
ultimate detection impossible. In other words,
it would have to project an image just beyond*

the belief structure of the target society. It
would have to disturb and reassure at the
same time, exploiting both the gullibility of
the zealots and the narrow-mindedness of
the debunkers. This is exactly what the
UFO phenomenon does. (14)

Some contemporary Roman Catholic theologians are now challenging the idea that belief in extraterrestrials is in any way contradictory to faith in God. On the contrary, they claim, their faith only confirms that God has not limited life to Earth, but has spread it out through the cosmos. The Vatican has been keen to promote itself as being at the forefront of astronomy and other sciences, maintaining several major astronomical observatories and a large number of radio telescopes. One of the Vatican's leading exorcists, and a close friend of Pope John Paul lI, Monsignor Corrado Balducci, observed that "The existence of these beings is real. We can't have doubts."(15) Balducci has also told reporters on a number of occasions that there has already been contact between humans and extraterrestrials.

Monsignor Balducci should not be considered a rogue voice making statements that might be at odds with the Vatican's teachings. As early as 2005, Vatican astronomer Guy Consolmango declared that the Roman Catholic Church believed humanity would discover intelligent life beyond Earth. When questions were raised about this, the Vatican's chief astronomer, Father Jose Gabril Funes, in 2008 assured the laity that belief in extraterrestrial life does not contradict the Christian faith. It is almost impossible to imagine that those working in such high profile positions in the Vatican could make such statements without receiving official approval. What appears to have been taking place is the Vatican's steady positioning itself for a post-disclosure world. This was confirmed when Pope Francis said:

He created beings and allowed them to
develop according to the internal laws that
he gave to each one, so that they were able
to develop and to arrive at their fullness of
being. He gave autonomy to the beings of
the universe at the same time at which he
assured them of his continuous presence,
giving being to every reality.(16)

In the same speech to the Pontifical Academy of Sciences, Pope Francis said that not only would alien visitors be welcome in Roman Catholic churches, but that he would seek to have them baptised. Such endorsement makes many assumptions (all of which we will show to be false), not least of which is that science is capable of understanding and explaining the UFO phenomenon. Amongst UFO researchers, such statements are seen as a sign that the "establishment" (church, government and military) knows more than it is admitting, and that it is slowly preparing the public for the moment of full disclosure.

UFOs are a sign of the post-Christian age that western culture has entered. The new religious consciousness that embraces eastern cults is no more than superstition, and UFOs fit easily into this. Roman Catholic theologians have a long history of following where ever science leads them, even spawning a new branch of their thinking, called exotheology: the theology of outer space. This is in keeping with the heretical "visionary" Emanuel Swedenborg who taught that the universality of the Church is inclusive of other life forms, and that union with Christ does not in any way require faith in Him.

The NASA philosopher Steven Dick has developed these themes and inevitably it leads to blasphemy. He argues that we should be open to the possibility that:

In a biological universe full of life, God may be a highly evolved super-intelligence, a natural rather than a supernatural entity, and non-anthropocentric in the sense that humans would be only one of many intelligent species and not the most highly evolved. In a post-biological universe, cultural evolution may have produced artificial intelligence, the most highly evolved version of which might have many of the properties of what we call God.(17)

Dick postulates that life is a "normal part" of what he calls "cosmic evolution". Nothing special, and certainly not dependent on a divine Creator. Once the philosophy of evolution is applied to a question, it seems anything is possible, including a

235

god-like artificial intelligence. The possibilities go even further, with many researchers, UFO witnesses and even academics, suggesting that extraterrestrials may be the saviours of mankind.

Dr. Young-hae Chi , an instructor in Korean at Oxford's Oriental Institute, wrote on April 17th 2019 that alien species may be living amongst us, inter-breeding in such a way that may enable mankind to avert ecological disaster.(18) According to his hypothesis, the aliens have come to share our biosphere, and consequently must prevent us from inflicting climate change on the world for their own survival. In an interview with the student campus newspaper promoting his book, he declared "Judging from the way the ETs are acting, they have a better view of our future". Chi says that the super-intelligent creatures are able to produce more capable hybrid offspring with humans which will be able to lead humanity away from its destructive path. Despite his research, the professor admits he is yet to find evidence to support his theories.

While this may appear to the majority of readers as a silly example, it demonstrates how open to these ideas our culture is becoming, since such a pronouncement would surely have once jeopardised someone's academic career. In his book *Dimensions*, Jacques Vallée labels this thinking as "the salvation myth", and presents an argument similar to Carl Jung's theory about how human psychology responds to perceived global destruction. Importantly he reminds his readers to ask themselves why they would be willing to jump aboard a vehicle on the promise of salvation from beings who have deceived and manipulated them. Vallée describes many contactees who claim to be "channelling" messages from the aliens which often offer reassurance and promises of technological solutions to the world's problems. This has long been a feature of UFO belief, from Bob Lazar's accounts of unknown energy sources (observed, he says while working at Area 51) to Dr Steven Greer's claims that governments are concealing the gift of free energy (that could revolutionise life on earth) in order to protect the interests of fossil fuel companies.

These ideas are really a result of belief in evolution. Extraterrestrials are not only believed to be more technologically advanced, but are seen as having developed beyond all the limitations of mankind. The materialism and atheism that invests all hope in the physical sciences has developed a fantasy about how the inventive capacity of intelligent life can solve all questions, even those that do not have a scientific answer. Spiritual evolution is assumed to parallel technological advancement, and since UFO researchers believe that alien life may have had a head start of millions of years on the evolution of life on Earth, it follows that they should also be imbued with the wisdom so often lacking in mankind.

There is, however, another important aspect as to how so many people should have fallen into this delusion. Contemporary man not only sees the wonders of technology and feels a sense of progress, but is trained through movies and literature to adopt a world view and his place within the cosmos that makes extraterrestrial neighbours an inevitability to him. So let us look in detail at how the spirit of science fiction is so crucial in the understanding of UFOs.

Endnotes
1 – Kiel, John, *UFO: Operation Trojan Horse*. New York, 1970 Chapter 12 "Space Jokers"
2 – Steiger made this claim in *The Star People*, Berkley Publishing Group, 1986
3 – Good, Timothy, *Alien Base*, Arrow Books Ltd, 1998, p.204
4 – ibid. Good, p.283
5 – ibid. Good, p.319
6 – ibid. Good, p.328
7 – ibid. Good, p.407

8 – ibid. Good, p.409

9 – ibid. Good, p.431

10 – ibid. Good, p.260

11 – ibid. Good, p.402

12 – Vallee, Jacques, *Messengers of Deception: UFO Contacts and Cults*, Daily Grail Publishing, 2008, p.20

13 – Ockels, Wubbo, details of his open letter can found at https://www.dutchnews.nl/news/2014/05/hollands_first_astronaut_dies/

14 – Vallee, Jacques, Confrontations, p.46

15 - Monsignor Corrado Balducci in an interview available online at https://www.youtube.com/watch?v=sdqn-77qija

16 – Pope Francis speaking about the harmony of faith and science to the Pontifical Academy of Sciences. http://www.ncregister.com/daily-news/pope-francis-lauds-benedict-xvis-emphasis-on-harmony-of-faith-and-science/#ixzz3HSmxPKb7

17 – Dick, Steven J., *Cosmotheology Revisited: Theological Implications of Extraterrestrial Life.* NASA Chief History Office, U.S. Naval Observatory, Washington.

18 – Chi, Dr. Young-hae *Alien Visitations and the End of Humanity*

Chapter Sixteen – The Spirit of Science Fiction

The genre of science fiction in literature, radio, cinema and television has its roots in the scientific revolution of the Seventeenth Century when advances in fields such as physics and astronomy ignited all kinds of fantasies amongst writers and artists. Some scholars argue that the roots of the genre lie in ancient epics and poems, such as *Beowulf* and even earlier in Ovid's *Metamorphoses*, but these only include elements of fantasy, and are not something we will consider here. Similarly the Hindu epic *Ramayana*, which dates back to the Fourth Century B.C. includes flying machines that can leave the Earth's atmosphere, but the purpose of this text is a religious one, and it does not draw on scientific knowledge to create its myth. In Sixteenth Century Europe, the Enlightenment began to transform cultures and man's sense of himself, and in works such as *Utopia* by the humanist Thomas Moore, we begin to see how the belief in progress affected political philosophy. Moore created the fantasy of a society that has become perfect for the inhabitants of an island, and the title *Utopia* not only entered everyday use but remained a theme for many subsequent science fiction works. However, it was in what became known as the Age Of Reason(1) that advances in science led writers to speculate on where technology and scientific discovery might lead humanity. In 1634 Johanne Kepler wrote *The Dream* (*Somnium*), which describes a journey to the moon, and which many later writers, including Carl Sagan and Isaac Asimov, identify as the first real work of science fiction. Kepler's themes inspired others to develop his ideas, and in 1752 Voltaire wrote about space journeys that led to encounters with alien people who are more advanced than humanity (in *Micromégas*).

It was in the Nineteenth Century that the genre had a greater cultural impact. In 1818 Mary Shelley published her story *Frankenstein*, which created many of the archetypes (such as a scientist who is going beyond the limits of acceptable science, and the threat of a monster) and though it is recognised as a gothic novel, it assured writers and publishers that this kind of material was popular with readers. Eighteen years after *Frankenstein*, the novel *Predki Kalimerosa: Aleksandr Filippovich Makedonskii* (*The Forebears of Kalimeros: Alexander, son of Philip of Macedon*), written by Alexander Veltman, was the first piece of literature to explore the idea of time travel, and is generally recognised as the first Russian work of science fiction.

All of this really set the stage for what was to come. In a period of five years Jules Verne created stories that encapsulate many of the themes we see in all the science fiction that was to follow: in 1864

241

he published *Journey to the Centre of the Earth*, in 1865 *From The Earth To The Moon* and in 1869 *Twenty Thousand Leagues Under The Sea*. Verne set his stories around technology that seemed realistic and potentially achievable based on what was currently available, and as a result found huge success. By 1895 H.G. Wells was developing many of Verne's themes and wrote *The Time Machine*. Wells used his writing to promote his political and philosophical beliefs, such as Darwinian evolution and Fabian socialism. There are also hints of eugenics (the control of the different human groups through breeding and conditioning) and he presented societies where, through the victory of technology, money has been eradicated in favour of more "advanced" means of exchange.

In 1898 H.G. Wells created the myth of alien invaders from outer space in *War Of The Worlds*, a piece of fiction that both drew on speculation about our Martian neighbours, but also helped the possibility gain wider acceptance. It was through Orson Wells' radio broadcast of the story in 1938 as part of his series The Mercury Theatre of the Air, that the urban myth developed suggesting that thousands of people had become hysterical after believing the drama was actually a news report of alien invasion (writers such as Jay Dyer argue that the panic was real, and was a Rockerfeller-funded psychological operation). From this point there were countless examples of cheap science fiction dramas and literature being produced to cash in on its popularity, and it is certainly no coincidence that

242

UFO experiences began to be interpreted in terms of extraterrestrial encounters. Similarly, government propaganda and disinformation departments realised how useful the myth of alien visitors could be for both maintaining a perceived danger or threat amongst the general population, and as a distraction when advanced aircraft were seen by the public.

Many writers who were not associated with the genre wrote science fiction stories, such as Edgar Allen Poe (a trip to the moon in *The Unparalleled Adventure of One Hans Pfaall*) and Jack London (encounters with aliens in *The Red One* and germ warfare in *The Unparalleled Invasion*). However, science fiction found a much larger audience in 1926 through *Amazing Stories* magazine, published by Hugo Gernsback (real name Gernsbacher). This was the first magazine dedicated to the genre, providing a forum for writers to explore new concepts and visions of the future. Gernsback went on to publish two other science fiction magazines, *Science Wonder Stories* and *Air Wonder Stories*, but it was his first magazine that captured public attention. Alongside stories that were utter fantasy, Gernsback encouraged writers to base their stories in what he considered "hard science", and he was known to see the magazine as a means of educating people about the possibilities that science could offer mankind. In other words, he used his position to promote ideas which he hoped would find acceptance in the broader culture.

The year after *Amazing Stories* was first published, the Austrian-German-American filmmaker Friedrich "Fritz" Lang released the movie *Metropolis.* This was an important development in science fiction, a film that cost five million Reichsmarks and took seventeen months to film; it is recognised as the first serious science fiction movie. It presents a vision of a future dystopia and includes a robot called the Maschinenmensch (which means machine-human) which continues to appear on the covers of music albums and was clearly the model on which C3PO in Star Wars was based. It is worth noting, even before we begin to analyse some of the imagery and messages of science fiction movies, that in one of the famous scenes in the film, the robot's "throne" is placed before a large inverted pentagram.

As the Twentieth Century moved on, science fiction writers began to include themes of alienation and positioned their characters as appearing isolated within strange cultures and environments. In the late 1930s a group of science fiction writers emerged known as the Futurians, which included names such as Isaac Asimov, Damon Knight, Donald A. Wollheim, Frederik Pohl and James Blish. Their goal was to celebrate the achievements of science and to promote the sense of progress that science promised. Famously, in 1948 George Orwell published *Nineteen Eighty Four* and a sub-genre appeared, warning of our potential enslavement by totalitarian political systems.

The impact of these writers and the extent to which their ideas were being taken seriously was demonstrated during the Second World War. The United States and British governments invited science fiction writers to suggest ideas for new technology. These were then used as leaks to the Axis powers as a means of disinformation, and included outlandish explanations for the Foo Fighters. By the end of the war, the bombing of Hiroshima and Nagasaki brought the realisation that technology could bring unimaginable destruction, and Isaac Asimov remarked that with the dropping of the atomic bombs, science fiction now had a new credibility because people could see the enormity of what man was capable.

The post-war period saw an enormous outpouring of science fiction. Many classic movies appeared during what has become known as the golden era of science fiction, including titles such as *Invasion of The Body Snatchers*, *Forbidden Planet*, *The Day The Earth Stood Still* and *The Thing from Another World*. The genre appeared in many new magazines and cheap paperbacks, and with the appearance of television, viewers were introduced to the likes of *Quatermas*, *Flash Gordon* and *Buck Rogers* (which had previously appeared in cinemas).

The 1960s brought a new status for science fiction. At the start of the decade the respected British writer Kingsley Aimis published *New Maps*

From Hell in which he examined the literary merits of the genre. Five years later Frank Herbert published *Dune*, which was viewed as a respectable piece of writing (no doubt in part because of its great length) in which he explored political and religious ideas. The 1960s also saw the arrival of *Star Trek*, which presented a future humanity where technology has freed us from the limits of Earth to wander and explore a godless universe. By the end of the decade such major films as *2001: A Space Odyssey* and *Planet of The Apes* were released, the first of which we shall mention in more detail below.

Throughout the 1970s and 80s, science fiction continued to reflect the political and social changes in ordinary life, by placing them in future settings or by creating potential imagined outcomes, often with extreme results (such as the wastelands of *Mad Max*). With the development of digital manipulation and creation of imagery (CGI) many contemporary movies have been able to place their characters in increasingly alien environments, and this in turn has affected many writers' imaginations. We will now question the extent to which this genre has been used to manipulate public perception, particularly with reference to UFOs, and where we can find examples of this in specific movies. We will then consider how the spirit of science fiction affects the worldview of so many people and contributes to the interpretation of UFO encounters.

We will begin with *2001: A Space Odyssey*, because it is one of the movies dealing so openly with philosophical issues. Stanley Kubrick presents us with a Darwinian universe where ape men are given a boost in their evolution by the presence of a monolith which transforms them into being able to control the world around them. An image of planetary alignment informs the viewer that a new aeon is beginning, and the ape men who are involved in a primitive resource war with another tribe, are able to become the stronger group by employing weapons to beat their rivals to death (survival of the fittest). Kubrick is making it very clear that this first evolutionary change is a shift to being able to employ weapons to defeat an enemy, and that human consciousness is a product of this evolutionary shift. The monolith has the same dimensions as a cinema screen (in Arthur C. Clarke's script the monolith taught through video images) and it has been suggested by the likes of the cultural commentator Jay Dyer, that Kubrick may be showing us that he himself is trying to change our consciousness through his movies. A further point worth noting is that monoliths play a key role in Masonic imagery. In the movie, when the astronauts discover a monolith on the moon, they are struck down by a choir of demonic voices which is leading mankind to the next stage of their development on one of the moons of Jupiter. We see an ongoing evolution portrayed which reaches its climax as the main character is taken through a

247

series of transformations leading him to become a "star child" observing earth from space.

Kubrick was thoroughly convinced of the inevitability of life on other planets, "It's reasonable to assume that there are countless billions of such planets where life has arisen"(2) he conjectured, and he went on to postulate what he considered the inevitable result:

Can you imagine the evolutionary
development that much older life forms
have taken? They may have progressed
from biological species, which are fragile
shells for the mind at best, into immortal
machine entites – and then, over
innumerable eons, they could emerge from
the chrysalis of matter transformed into beings
of pure energy and spirit. Their
potentialities would be limitless and
their intelligence ungraspable by humans.(3)

Even if we bear in mind that film directors are likely to say outlandish things when promoting their latest movie, Kubrick's own beliefs that underpin the themes of the film are there to see. It is interesting to note how far from science he is happy to stray, expressing fantasies that are dressed up in pseudo-scientific theories, but which amount to nothing more than new age-type fancies.

Kubrick's comment about "machine entities" is worthy of note. Both he and Clarke expressed ideas about artificial intelligence (A.I.) eventually assuming the place of God. In 2001 we see the HAL computer system recognising the human crew members as a threat to its objective, and utterly expendable (an idea taken even further in *The Terminator* movies). And Clark, in his story *The Final Query* explored this theme further, stating the idea that man's purpose may be to create god in the form of super-efficient computers. At the heart of both this idea, and Kubrick's notion of aliens evolving into limitless intelligence as the real deity of this cosmos, is advanced intelligence and nothing more. Clarke stated this quite openly in his sequel *3001: The Final Odyssey,* where God is discovered to be an ancient A.I. system that has created the world and man.

In the 1960 movie version of *The Time Machine* we see the same themes. From his crystal powered machine, the scientist witnesses how Darwinian evolution results in humanity being divided into different groups, and that society has relinquished its habits of marriage and family. Wells also said to reporters that he intentionally described the future people as having a genderless appearance, since he believed that gender distinction is an unnecessary and primitive feature. The image is of a humanity that has no claim to a special place in the order of the universe, certainly not created in God's image. This meaninglessness to man's existence is only amplified by films like *Alien* (1979), which reveal man's insignificance as he drifts through limitless space. It is ironic that so much science fiction should reduce the relevance of man to an accident of cosmic chemistry and physics, while simultaneously preaching that true meaning and purpose can only be found through man's own reason and technological creativity. We could argue that it is not man that is presented as capable of greatness, but science.

Steven Spielberg has directed two major movies that have profoundly affected the direction science fiction has travelled: *Close Encounters of The Third Kind* (1977) and *E.T.* (1982). While so many previous films of the genre depicted extraterrestrials as a threat, in these two Spielberg convinced his audience that aliens were to be welcomed. While anxiety about an alien invasion can be damaging to people, by shifting public opinion into believing that aliens will come as friends, Spielberg only made believers even more vulnerable. Spielberg's cuddly aliens bring advanced technology, of course, and in both movies chosen people are contacted because they are special in some way.

Close Encounters begins with crowds of Hindu worshippers singing the tune taught to them by the UFO. As they sing the notes they appear to be saying "Yahweh", the Hebrew pronunciation of the name of God revealed to Moses. Spielberg has humanity meeting with the UFOs on a mountain top (Devil's Tower), just as so many Old Testament prophets met with God in high places, and also the Apostles who witnessed Christ's transfiguration on Mount Tabor. In both films the lead characters are alienated from their families; In *Close Encounters* the protagonist drives his family away with his UFO obsession, and in *E.T.* young

Eliot, the boy who encounters the alien, is an outsider to the fun and game playing enjoyed by others. This is a common feature of many films aimed at children; there are, for example, many characters in Disney films who lose their parents (even in films like *Dumbo* and *Bambi*). Jay Dyer proposes that this may be an indication of wider themes, once more pointing to the Marxist theory of alienation.(4) The alien in *E.T.* possesses magic powers and is able to levitate objects and himself, and at key moments of the film places his glowing finger on the boy's forehead, which in Hindu texts is the location of the third eye. Spielberg even endows the alien with the power of resurrection, presented in a sentimental moment when the boy's love for him starts his heart up again. The aliens of *Close Encounters* also possess occult powers, transmitting telepathic images to those they have contacted in order to draw them to their meeting place. Only those courageous enough to answer the call will be rewarded with the revelation of the mothership at the film's climax.

In both of these movies the aliens appear as the small grey beings that have now become a common image in western culture. Fear of the greys, the movies tell us, is to be abandoned. However, it is important to remember that the classic grey alien appears exactly as the Satanist Aleister Crowley described and painted the spirit being he claimed to have had as a guide.(5)

More recently science fiction has pursued the idea that man owes his existence to alien life which has been brought to Earth. With NASA scientists talking about panspermia(6) the myth is given a scientific plausibility, regardless of there being no scientific evidence for it whatsoever. In the original *Alien* movies, themes of biological evolution, survival and existential crisis are explored within a hostile universe where both other lifeforms and human greed are the threat. The cosmos is presented as being utterly nihilistic, with man shown as one struggling life form battling another. Beyond survival, there is nothing. It is worthy of note that the logo worn by crew members of the spaceship "Nostromo" is an image of the winged disc Horus, from Egyptian mythology. In 2013, director Ridley Scott released the prequel to the original Alien film, called *Prometheus*. Whereas before he was content to portray a godless universe as a backdrop to the main story, this time theological concepts become a central theme, with the creation of man playing an important part of the story. The opening sequence shows an alien, from a race nicknamed "The Engineers", who drinks a black liquid that causes his body to crumble, and so seed his DNA into an Eden-like Earth. Later we learn that the process that produced man is a biological weapon. Replacing God with the "Engineers" as our creators, we see clear links with ideas of Freemasonry, which calls the creator the "Great Architect".

Science fiction literature and drama communicates a philosophy, often without explicitly stating what that philosophy is about.

First, it rejects traditional religion, the societies and cultures portrayed exist in a "post-Christian" universe. The secular outlook of its characters does on occasions admit a spirituality, but this is almost always drawn from eastern mysticism. For example in *Star Wars*, the Jedi have a temple where they learn the ways of an unseen force that guides and influences them: and even produces a virgin birth in the case of Anakin Skywalker. But it is not personal, it has no other name, and within it there is an evil aspect, the dark side, which is the equal of the good side. Therefore, we may say the philosophy inherent in science fiction is intended to reflect man's rejection of traditional religious values.

For the Orthodox Christian, at the centre of life and the cosmos is God. But in the Godless universe of sci-fi it is man's reasoning powers that become the all-important aspect of existence. Science fiction promotes a belief that man himself will continue to evolve, and so it is the very mind of man through his technological advancements, that imposes meaning on reality. In his advanced state, the man of the future is portrayed as having evolved beyond many of the limitations that we experience, often even beyond his own personal identity. Just as "the force" of *Star Wars* is impersonal, so too many works in this genre see man as trying to move beyond the frailties of his individuality: many stories even explore how such remnants of our humanity come into conflict with this new way of being. The impersonal is seen as an evolutionary goal which once more reflects the goal of eastern beliefs such as some schools of Buddhism. It is a desire for transcendence.

One of the dangers of this philosophy is that the stories often involve themes of telepathy and other psychic phenomena. In the Godless reality of science fiction, what Orthodox Christianity would reject as occult the evolved future man embraces as being aspects of his higher self. Another common theme is the arrival of aliens who enter human beings to take control of them. There are a number of episodes of *Star Trek* as well as movies, where this is the storyline. Orthodox Christians see the portrayal of demonic possession in these dramas, and the all-powerful beings encountered on other planets wield the influence of sorcery and magic under pseudo-scientific terminology. While science fiction writers make the claim to be exploring where science can lead us, in fact they are merely retreating to the occultism of previous centuries, and presenting a non-Christian world view. In keeping with this philosophy, the idea of advanced saviours who will arrive to solve our problems is reinforced. But science fiction also warns that even if an alien saviour doesn't appear from the skies, humanity had better listen to the warnings of scientists if we are to avoid the potential apocalypses that is of our own making.

In one sense, Dr Valee is right, the UFO phenomenon is a factor in the changing human consciousness. As Father Seraphim Rose states, they are part of a bigger picture, where many different psychic and occult experiences are becoming more common. Strange events are contributing to the shift in man's belief patterns, and Father Seraphim reminds us that it is the same unseen forces at work that have been described throughout human history. In his work Orthodoxy and the Religion of the Future, Father Seraphim warns that UFOs are a sign of mediumistic techniques that the demons have used throughout time as a way of drawing people into occultism. Therefore the spirit of science fiction is evidence that modern culture has become so far removed from Orthodox Christianity that it is no longer able to identify what was obvious to Christians of the past. The repeated message from extraterrestrials is often that we are to prepare ourselves for the one who comes: antichrist. As Bishop Ignatius Bryanchaninov warned, the ability to experience true miracles is diminishing amongst men while the thirst for signs and wonders only grows. In this condition, man has never been so vulnerable to demonic deception. Technical developments create awe and wonder amongst many people, and the gadgets and telephones that are ubiquitous amongst westerners maintain an ongoing expectation of what science will give us next. Science fiction has determined this expectation, guiding many to accept the teachings of Freemasonry and Hindu mysticism. As Jay Dyer writes:

With the rise of the Royal Society and
its masonic atomistic dogmatism, the focal
point of empirical scientism was able

*to evangelise the earth with its new
paradigm, pragmatic scientism where
perpetual becoming has cancelled all notions
of being.*(7)

It is, as Dyer goes on to say, a pursuit of progress that has no ethical bounds. Transhumanism and the manipulation of our DNA is no longer fiction but science fact. Elon Musk has announced a device that plugs into the brain to stimulate its perception, thousands of people in Sweden are volunteering to become microchipped, and the most of the world was persuaded to accept an experimental RNA treatment for the flu. Whether so many people would be willing to accept these measures if they had not first seen them played out in movies is impossible to say. But now that friendly, advanced aliens have been established in people's consciousness, we can only wonder at how willing they would be to accept news that the UFOs have finally revealed themselves; especially if they came with a solution to this year's crisis, such as global warming.

A number of times I have made reference to the demonic nature of UFOs, but so far without any clear explanation for this belief. In our next chapter we will examine exactly why Orthodox Christians believe such phenomena is to be rejected, and how it fits into the teaching of the Church.

Endnotes

1 – "The Age Of Reason" or "Enlightenment" was a European philosophical movement in the seventeenth and eighteenth centuries that elevated man's reason above all other means of acquiring knowledge, including divine revelation.

2 – Kubrick, Stanley, in an interview with *Playboy*, quoted in What Did Kubrick Have To Say About What 2001 Means? found at http://www.krusch.com/kubrick/Q12.html

3 – ibid. Kubrick

4 – Dyer, Jay, *Esoteric Hollywood Sex, Cults and Symbols In Film*, Trine day LLC, 2016, p.139

5 – Aleister Crowley (1875 -1947) was a British occultist, magician, founder of the religion of Thelema, and who identified himself as the prophet entrusted with guiding humanity into the *Æon of Horus*. He admitted to have participated in Satanic rituals.

6 – Panspermia is the hypothesis that life exists throughout the Universe and is distributed by space dust, meteoroids, asteroids, comets, planetoids, and also by alien visitation.

7 – op cit. Dyer, Jay, *Esoteric Hollywood*, p.113

Chapter Seventeen – The Truth Behind The Deception

After concerning ourselves with a number of worldly voices and secular perspectives, we will now see how the UFO phenomenon is to be understood by Orthodox Christians. As Father Seraphim Rose tells us, there are countless examples of demonic manifestation that conform precisely to UFO encounters, such as in the lives of St. Anthony the Great and St. Cyprian.(1) Father Seraphim demonstrates how the demons have adapted their appearance and behaviour to fit with contemporary man's understanding of science and space, and what the universe is likely to reveal to him. Where once the demons presented themselves as angels, now, in a culture that has lost its connection with the Christian faith, they take on the form of extraterrestrials. But the purpose remains the same, regardless of what they pretend to be: to create confusion and lead men away from God.

Modern man is experiencing the level of demonic activity experienced in the Eighteenth Century, but he is no longer equipped with Christian understanding and cannot interpret it properly. Modern researchers like Steven Greer recognise the psychic nature of the phenomenon, but instead of understanding its danger, they embrace occult practices in order to intensify the experience. UFO sightings are so common that many secular scientists are turning to occultism to understand the phenomenon, which leads to occult practices gaining a new kind of legitimacy that entices yet more people: we can state as our first argument that UFOs are drawing many modern people into forbidden practices. Without the support of a Christian culture or personal upbringing, these individuals are utterly vulnerable to the trick.

Many secular scientists have abandoned notions of good and evil and consider the empirical scientific method a suitable means of examining the spiritual realm. The error of believing that they can approach such things with an objective, neutral position provides the demons with an opportunity to deliver to them all kinds of signs that can satisfy their studies. Imagining himself to be at the peak of human evolution and scientific discovery, contemporary man has in fact entered a new era of superstition, embracing fantasies of alien saviours from outer space.

It is not only Orthodox Christianity that recognises how the UFO phenomenon is deeply rooted in psychic and occult activities. The U.S. Government Printing Office published a report in 1969 that was prepared by the Library of Congress for the U.S. Air Force Office of Scientific Research, it stated:

Many of the UFO reports now being published

in the popular press recount alleged incidents
that are strikingly similar to demonic possession
and psychic phenomena which have long
been known to theologians.(2)

In the report we learn that those who believe that they have come into contact with a UFO and aliens, describe experiencing the same emotional and psychological effects of those who explore the occult realm and claim to have encountered demons. Those who say they have had direct contact with the occupants of the "craft" often suffer much worse symptoms that resemble possession.

Father Seraphim observed the same similarities. In 1975 he wrote:

People often have strange dreams just
before seeing UFOs, or hear knocks on the
door when no one is there, or have
strange visitors afterwards; some
witnesses receive telepathic messages from
UFO occupants.(3)

Again, even Dr Hynek admits that UFOs are "a phenomenon that undoubtedly has physical effects but also has the attributes of the psychic world."(4)

In response to this information, it is necessary to ask two questions: how can demons leave physical evidence of their activities, and where does Orthodox Christian tradition support such ideas. As we shall see, there is a huge body of material explaining exactly where and how the demons exist, but first let us address this issue of the nature of the demons.

Though we cannot completely comprehend or define their nature, we can describe the activity of angels from patristic and biblical sources. Throughout the Bible we see angels acting as God's messengers, and appearing in forms that do not completely overwhelm the men to whom they reveal themselves. Demons too take on many forms, but the purpose of their transformation is not to protect us, but in order that they may deceive us, and perform signs and miracles through the power of "the prince of the air" (*Ephesians* 2 v2). Blessed Augustine tells us that:

The nature of demons is such that, through
the sense perception belonging to the aerial
body, they readily surpass the
perception possessed by earthly bodies, and
in speed too, because of the superior mobility
of the aerial body, they incomparably excel
not only the movements of men and of beasts
but even the flight of birds.(6)

Today we might add to Blessed Augustine's comment that they exceed the capabilities of fighter jets. The ability to transform themselves is also confirmed in Saint Paul's *Second letter to the Corinthians* when he says "Satan is transformed into an angel of light, and his ministers as the servants of righteousness."(7) Glowing lights in the sky that move at impressive speeds are clearly something demons can become. But this still leaves the question of radar signals and physical impressions left on the ground and on people.

As a result of The Fall, our human bodies and their senses have lost the capacity to perceive the spiritual reality for which they were created. As Saint Ignatius Brianchaninov writes:

In this condition of darkness, by reason of their extreme crudeness and coarseness, the bodily senses are incapable of communion with spirits, they do not see them, do not hear them, do not sense them. Thus, the blunted axe is no longer capable of being used according to its purpose. The holy spirits avoid communion; while the fallen spirits who have drawn us into their fall, have mingled with us and, as the more easily to hold us in their captivity.(8)

Father Seraphim cites the example of the Archangel Raphael who travelled with Tobias for weeks without anyone suspecting he wasn't a physical man.(9) Similarly Abraham believed that the three angels who visited him were mortal men, and in both stories the angels supported this impression by eating and drinking. Therefore we see that even God's angels adapt their appearance in order that men may see and communicate with them. This does not, however, mean that angels and demons have bodies that conform to the crudeness of men's bodies, but neither does it mean that these spirits share in the kind of spiritual existence that alone can be attributed to God. There are degrees of material density, and since angels and demons are creatures like us, they are not pure spirit as only God has revealed Himself. Father Seraphim Rose argues in *The Soul After Death*, that it is heretical to believe that demons are pure spirit and cannot interact with the material world. The physical signs of UFO "landings" are often claimed as evidence that the phenomenon is not occult or supernatural in nature, but such a claim is based on a false idea of demons and how they act. We must remind non-Orthodox readers that what we know of angels helps us to understand the demons because the latter were once part of the heavenly host. As we read in the twelfth verse of the twelfth chapter of the *Book of Revelation*:

And there was a war in Heaven: Michael and his angels fought against the dragon; and the dragon fought and his angels, and prevailed not; neither was their place found anymore in Heaven. And the great dragon was cast out, that old serpent, called the Devil, and Satan, which deceiveth the whole world; he was cast out into the earth, and his angels were cast out with him.

For those familiar with Orthodox Christian tradition, it is no surprise that the demons should attempt to deceive mankind in the skies, for it is above us that the demons dwell. We will now present some of the patristic and biblical writings that demonstrate the truth of this reality. Saint Ignatius Brianchaninov states:

The space between heaven and earth, the whole azure expanse of the air which is visible to us under the heavens, serves as the dwelling for the fallen angels who have been

263

cast down from Heaven.(10)

Bishop Brianchaninov was a Russian theologian who died in 1867. His statement may appear shocking to some who are not familiar with this teaching, but even non-Orthodox Christians should have encountered this teaching in the Bible. In his *Letter to the Ephesians*, Saint Paul describes the fallen demons as "spirits of wickedness under the heavens."(11) Four chapters later in the same letter he writes:

For our fight is not against flesh and blood, but against principalities, against the powers, against the world-rulers of the darkness of this age, against the spirits of wickedness under the heavens.(12)

Here we must distinguish between how the Orthodox Church understands these biblical texts as opposed to Protestant or Roman Catholic interpretations. The Church teaches that the only way we can grasp the meaning of the Bible is through the writings of the Church Fathers. Therefore, if a Protestant argues that these quotations do not indicate that the demons inhabit the aerial realms, then they must deny the very foundation on which biblical exegesis has been based throughout the history of the Church. So let us consider exactly what the Fathers said about this. Many of their statements come in the context of things they wrote about the departure of the soul after death.

Saint John Chrysostom wrote a commentary on the *Epistle to the Ephesians*, and explaining the quotations above he wrote:

Here again he (the Apostle Paul) means
that Satan occupies the space under Heaven,
and that the incorporeal powers are spirits of
the air, under his operation.(13)

Speaking about the journey of the soul after death, Saint John also writes that we will need the protection of our Guardian Angel against "the invisible dignities and powers and world rulers of this air who are called persecutors."(14)

Saint Athanasios warned that:

The devil, the enemy of our race, having
fallen from Heaven, wanders about our lower
atmosphere, and there bearing rule over
his fellow spirits.(15)

In the same work, Saint Athanasius describes their activity in the lower atmosphere, he says they "work illusions" and that Christ came to "clear the air and prepare the way for us up to Him."(16) Christ's death on the cross was in the very air where the demons are present. He was lifted up to confront and abolish the fruit of their work, which is death. Saint Athanasius writes:

Our Lord Jesus Christ, Who took upon Him
to die for all, stretched forth his hands,
not somewhere on the earth beneath, but in the
air itself...destroying the devil who was
working in the air.(17)

This understanding of the cross is reiterated by Saint Simeon the Myrrh-streamer in the Twelfth

Century who declared, "Let the cross bring you to stand blamelessly before Christ's throne, driving the aerial tax collectors away from you."(18)

Saint John Cassian, writing at the beginning of the Fifth Century says:

This air which is spread out between heaven and earth is so thick with spirits, which do not fly about in it quietly and aimlessly.(19)

This is an important point to remember when reflecting on the reality of UFOs. The demons do not simply dwell in the skies, but are active in their work of deception. Their movements are controlled and deliberate, exactly as witnesses describe seeing UFOs move. Saint Philotheos Kokkinos, Patriarch of Constantinople in the Fourteenth Century, also comments on this movement: "The devil, having fallen from the heavens with his evil spirits, is roaming about the air."(20)

Saint Makarios the Great of Egypt in the Fourth Century, presents us with a sobering warning:

There are rivers of dragons and mouths of lions and the dark forces under the heavens and fire that burns and crackles in all the members (such that the earth could never contain).(21)

In the Sixth Century, Saint Anastasios the Great, Abbot of Mount Sanai, described them as "the principalities and authorities – our bitter accusers of the air."(22) Nearly two hundred years earlier, Saint Isaiah of Scetis issued a similar warning when he wrote "Be concerned about how you will leave this body and pass the powers of darkness that will meet you in the air."(23)

Saint Nikodemos of the Holy Mountain, best known for his work compiling the texts of *The Philokalia*, reflecting on the expectation of those who have been obedient to Christ wrote:

When our soul departs from us, it will fly like a dove in freedom and joy into the heavens, without being inhibited whatsoever by the spirits lurking in the air.(24)

This is echoed by a more recent Athonite Archimandrite, Elder Aimilianos, Abbot of Simonos Petras Monastery, who died in 2019. He wrote "There are legions of demons occupying every last corner of the atmosphere, where God has granted them the right to exercise their rule."(25)

Saint John Klimakos in his book *The Ladder of Divine Ascent*, asks "Will our soul pass through the irresistible water of the spirits of the air?"(26)

Hieromartyr Daniel Sysoev of Moscow states clearly that:

Above the earth is the kingdom of Satan. Above the earth is the realm of the spirits beneath the heavens, a place where the devil rules. Sacred scripture speaks frankly about this, calling it "spiritual wickedness in high places (Eph.6v12).(27)

Metropolitan Hierotheos Vlachos of Nafpaktos once more confirms this teaching, he writes:

The devil is characterised as the prince of the power of the air because he is in the atmosphere and is constantly waging war on men.(28)

Archimandrite Panteleimon Nizhnik, who founded the monastery of Holy Trinity, Jordanville, and served there as abbot, describing our journey after death states:

The powers of darkness have established
particular seats of judgement and
particular watches, and through these the
souls pass and are tried during their rise
through the air. Throughout the space
between earth and heaven there watchfully
stand contingents of the fallen spirits.(29)

Saint Seraphim of Sarov, one of Russia's most beloved saints, confirms this teaching about the demons in the sky when he writes "The soul that is filled with love of God, at the time of departure from its body, does not fear the prince of the air."(30)

From the same period of time as Saint Seraphim, Saint Herman of Alaska was also declaring this teaching, he writes:

Although we do not have such grace as the
Apostles had, still our wrestling is against the
same fleshless principalities and powers, against
the rulers of the darkness of this age, against the
spirits of evil under heaven, who strive to
intercept and hold and prevent all travellers
toward our heavenly fatherland. (31)

Let us include just one more quotation to confirm this belief. It comes from Saint Nikolai Velimirovic, Bishop of Ochrid (who compiled *The Prologue from Ochrid*) who wrote:

According to the course of this world means
the way of sin; according to the prince of
the power of the air means following the will
of those chiefs of the devils that dwell in
the air...What is this power of the air,
my brethren? It is the order of evil spirits
that exist in constant movement in the air.
These spirits make the air a substance of
this earth.(32)

This is just a selection of the many saints and Church Fathers who teach that the space beneath the heavens is truly inhabited by demons. Reading these quotations we would expect the teaching to be found within the liturgical life of the Church, and that is precisely what we do find. In the Canon chanted at the departing of the soul we pray:

The prince of the air, the oppressor, the
tyrant who standeth on the dread paths,
the relentless accountant thereof, do
thou vouchsafe me who am departing from
the earth to pass, O Theotokos.(33)

In the Akathist to the Archangel Michael we pray "leave us not defenceless against the spirits of evil in the upper air." Similar prayers are found in the Akathist to Saint Sergius of Radonezh (attributed to Pachomius Logofet) and in the Akathist to Saint Photios, Patriarch of Constantinople.

Such belief is incomprehensible to the modern mind. But as Saint Theophan the Recluse tells us:

Physical evidence reveals nothing in
the atmosphere except for air with
some incidental strata of other

atmospheric bodies, while Divine
Revelation states that this is the area of the
aerial powers, of the spiritual wickedness in
high places who sleep neither day nor night
in their effort to harm us. The demons
encountered in the course of our lives hide
in secret, like a beast waiting to catch its
prey, attacking the soul suddenly.(34)

When we understand UFOs as manifestations of these aerial spirits, we are better able to make sense of much of their activity. So much of it, as we have shown earlier, is without meaning, confusing and often bizarre. The demons are not spoken of in terms of their power, but rather their influence. The Church has always understood them to be deceivers (Satan is the father of lies), and it is their capacity to deceive that makes them dangerous, since men may be led into delusion. Saint Anthony of the Desert instructed his disciples to ignore the visions created by demons, to crush them like scorpions under foot, since there is no truth in them. If the demons had real power they would not permit a single Orthodox Christian to go on living, and yet they manage only to threaten, frighten, confuse and mislead. Therefore we may speak of the only power they can have over us as being when we choose to submit to their will. Satan and his demons cannot destroy us, but they work to lead us into destroying ourselves. Our task is to protect ourselves from the deception in the air, Saint Symeon the New Theologian goes as far as to teach "the struggler of prayer should quite rarely look into the sky out of fear of the evil spirits in the air."(35)

Saint John Cassian reminds us that it is in His mercy that God has stripped us of the ability to perceive the demons above us. God also prevents them from entering and possessing us unless we choose to open ourselves to them through occult practices. They therefore seek to influence us through sinful desires and fantasies, but if we are foolish enough to try to acquire knowledge of them when they masquerade as visitors from other planets, we invite deception into ourselves. Any kind of "wisdom" or "help" that they offer is intended to lead us to perdition with them. Saint Ignatius Brianchaninov writes:

A general rule for all men is by no means to trust the spirits when they appear, not to enter into conversation with them, not to pay any attention to them, to acknowledge their appearance as a great and most dangerous temptation. At the time of this temptation one should direct one's mind and heart to God with a prayer for mercy and for deliverance from temptation.(36)

As Father Seraphim Rose recognised in the 1970s, where once it was necessary to have men meet in dark rooms for séances in order to have them commune with demons, all that is needed today is that they look up into the skies. The new superstitious consciousness leaves man in a spiritually passive condition, willing to believe in anything he sees above him: especially if it fills him with wonder and awe. In *The Gospel of Saint Luke* we are warned that "there shall be terrors and great signs from heaven" as Satan attempts to gain authority over mankind.(37)

Throughout history, Christians have been wary of any kind of strange phenomenon, knowing they were vulnerable to demonic action. Today even many Christians have rejected the existence of demons as something outdated and not worthy of their modern thinking and are not only curious about strange events, they actively seek them out. It is not only Roman Catholics who are looking for life elsewhere, but Protestants too. But as Seraphim Rose reminds us, there are indeed other life forms above us, in fact two: angels and demons. So long as man seeks out contact with such beings without the ascetical struggles of Orthodox Christianity he will only encounter demons, and they will present themselves in whatever form man's current philosophies make most acceptable: today that is as UFOs.

Endnotes

1 – Rose, Father Seraphim, *Orthodoxy And The Religion Of The Future*, St. Herman of Alaska Brotherhood, 1997, p.104

2 – Catoe, Lynn, *UFOs And Related Subjects: An Annotated Bibliography*, U.S. Government Printing Office, Washington, 1969

3 – op. cit. Rose, Seraphim, *Orthodoxy And The Religion of The Future*, p.97

4 – The Edge of Reality: Progress Report On J.A. Hynek and Jacques Vallee, Chicago 1975, p.259

5 – Vallee, Jacques, The Invisible College, Dulton, N.Y. 1975, p.p.197-198

6 - Blessed Augustine, "The Divination of Demons", Chapter 3 of *The Fathers Of The Church* Volume 27, p.426

7 – 2 Corinthians 11 v14-15

8 – Saint Ignatius Brianchaninov, *Collected Work*, Volume 3, p.8

9 – Rose, Father Seraphim, *The Soul After Death*, St. Herman of Alaska Brotherhood, 2009, p.26

10 – op. cit. Bishop Brianchaninov, p.132

11 – Ephesians 2 v2

12 – Ephesians 6 v12

13 – Saint John Chrysostom, Homilies On Ephesians, Homily 4, Volume 13, Grand Rapids, 1994, p.66

14 – Saint John Chrysostom, On Patience And Gratitude, *Collected Works*, Volume 3, Moscow 2011, p.427

15 – Saint Athanasius the Great, *On The Incarnation Of The Word*, Volume 4, Grand Rapids 1987, p.577

16 – ibid. Saint Athanasius, p.50

17 – ibid. Saint Athanasius, p.50

18 – Stefanov, Archimandrite Pavel, "Between Heaven and Hell: Toll-Houses of the Souls After Death in Slavonic Literature and Art", in *IKON: Journal of Iconographic Studies*, Volume 4, Rijeka, 2011, p.86

19 – Saint John Cassian, *The Conference*, New York, 1977, p.271

20 – Saint Philotheos Kokkinos, *Homily On The Elevation of the Honourable and Life-giving Cross*

21 - Saint Makarios the Great of Egypt, *The Fifty Spiritual Homilies*, "Homily 43", Mahwah, 1992, p.222

22 – Saint Anastasios the Great, *Beneficial Homily On the Deceased, cited in The Departure Of the Soul*, St Anthony's Greek Orthodox Monastery, 2017, p.171

23 – Saint Isaiah of Scetis, *Ascetic Discourses*, "Discourse 1", Kalamazoo, 2002, p.40

24 – Saint Nikodemus of the Holy Mountain, *Concerning Frequent Communion of the Immaculate Mysteries of Christ*, Thessaloniki, 2006, p.118

25 – Archimandrite Aimilianos, *Interpretation of the Ascetical Homilies of Abba Isaiah*, Athens, 2006, p.315

26 – Saint John Klimakos, *The Ladder Of Divine Ascent*, p.169

27 – Hieromartyr Daniel Sysoev, *Instructions For The Immortal*, Moscow, 2013, p.11

28 – Metropolitan Hierotheos Vlachos, *Life and Death*, Levadia, 1996, p.64

29 – Archimandrite Panteleimon Nizhnik, *Eternal Mysteries Beyond The Grave*, Jordanville, 2012, p.64

30 – *Saint Seraphim of Sarov, Little Russian Philokalia*, Volume 1, Platina, 1996, p.26

31 – *Saint Herman of Alaska, Little Russian Philokalia*, Volume 3, Platina, 1998, p.50

32 – Saint Nikolai Velimirovic, *The Prologue from Ochrid*, Volume 4, Birmingham, 1985, p.170

33 – Canon chanted at the departing of the soul at death, Ode IV, troparion 4

34 – Saint Theophan the Recluse, *Spiritual Heritage of Saint Theophan the Recluse*, "Rumination and Reflection: Precise Teachings", Moscow, 2007, p.70

35 – Saint Symeon the New Theologian, *The Philokalia*, in "The Three Forms of Heedfulness"

36 – op. cit. Saint Ignatius Brianchaninov, p.11

37 – Luke 21 v11

Chapter Eighteen – Conclusion

I began this book with a description of my wife's own experience of the UFO phenomenon as an explanation of why I had no doubts in its reality. I then presented a number of examples of UFO events to demonstrate that this is something many people have experienced, and is something that governments are taking seriously.

However, it is equally clear that a deliberate attempt has been made to mislead the public on this subject. This has involved issuing contradictory information (such as the various explanations for the events at Roswell) to planting intelligence agents in civilian UFO research groups in order to guide and monitor their activities. The "deception" in the title of this book refers to the demonic presentation of themselves as extraterrestrials. But a second form of deception has been taking place alongside it.

The fact that governments have been deliberately been concealing and misrepresenting the UFO phenomenon is something UFO researchers have recognised for a long time. It is a constant theme in their books and on their websites. The conclusion they have drawn from this is that political leaders have some corrupt motivation for keeping their contact with aliens a secret. This has been the argument from the likes of Steven Greer. As a consequence, UFO believers invest a great deal of psychological energy in the hope that one day the truth will be revealed, that "disclosure" will finally come.

I want to present an alternative possibility that are my own conclusions. As Orthodox Christians we know that some of the UFOs are actually demons. This reality will not have been overlooked by the many government investigations into the phenomenon, even if they do not fully understand the demonic nature. We can only guess at how those in power try to conform this knowledge to their own beliefs, but what we can be sure of is that they will be using the phenomenon in any way that favours their own agenda. The military invests unimaginable amounts of money developing and testing advanced aircraft, and maintaining the belief in UFOs creates a perfect cover story for when one of them is seen or photographed. With yet more footage of UFOs being released by the U.S. Navy in 2021, we see this second deception continuing, perpetuating the sense that something big is just around the corner.

The roots of the confusion modern man finds himself in have their roots twisting through many previous centuries. But in the medieval understanding of the universe, reality was God-centred, not man-centred. Even Augustine did not argue that God created the world for man because

He needed man, but as an expression of His love and wisdom. Pre-enlightenment thinkers have been falsely characterised as claiming that Christianity taught something which Copernicus corrected, whereas the truth is that what scientism rejected was not the truth of Christianity at all. In fact, it is the very belief that God created an ordered universe that has permitted Christian scientists through the ages to examine the physical world and study its laws precisely - because they believed (and believe) God made it this way. The conflict between faith and science on this issue is an illusion.

We must also note that while Aristotle taught that the cosmos itself is eternal, Christianity maintains that it is a creation of the eternal God, and that it exists within a limited framework of time. Modern science too, proposed until recently that there is a cyclical nature to the universe, unlike Christianity that has maintained that not only is time linear, but that it is heading to a definite end. These notions of time are important because they affect the way the physical universe is perceived and the expectations we have about what it might produce. Even in the past few hundred years, many prominent scientists anticipated finding life on the planets of our own solar system, and Kepler wrote that he believed that the moon's surface seemed to show evidence of intelligently constructed structures. These ideas were rejected once sufficient evidence was acquired. Similarly we see many astrobiologists expressing the same kinds of expectations about life on other planets: without the biblical foundation for understanding life on Earth, such conjecture inevitably follows. This is something we must grasp: scientists openly taught that life on Mars and the other planets of our solar system was something we should expect until evidence was found that was sufficient to confront and suppress this teaching. Today NASA continues to excite public opinion about life existing elsewhere, but with their robots now crawling over the surface of Mars, the expectation has begun to be downgraded to what that life may be, and the can has been kicked down the road again, with the focus turning to some of the moons orbiting the gas giants.

Another contemporary scientific philosophy is that of the possibility of multiple universes. This hypothesis is entirely unscientific, as we have shown, because it is impossible to falsify it as a theory since by definition all evidence will exist outside this universe. While it is offered as somehow rational and science-based, the belief in a Creator God can be interpreted from many aspects of the universe, and while others may be free to reject this interpretation, it is a belief that has a causal explanation of life, unlike the many universes theory.

In the post-Christian West, the promises of Humanistic materialism are proving empty. Men are searching for the truth of personal experience and so exposing themselves to a variety of occult practices. Meditation and yoga classes are available in schools, prisons, work places and even non-

Orthodox places of worship, and the acceptable face of witchcraft is found on chat-shows and in movies. Along with the spirit of the age, many western Christians are willing to experiment with practices that would once have been judged as satanic and avoided. It should be of no surprise that UFOs, once the interest of a few fringe groups, has now entered the mainstream, and the possibility of a dramatic sign from the heavens comes closer. As Saint Gregory the Great writes: "The spiritual world is moving closer to us, manifesting itself through visions and revelations."[1]

As we have seen, extraterrestrials are an accepted reality for western man because science fiction has provided the fantasies and imagery, technological advances have given him the reasoned expectation that space flight could happen, and evolution has built the philosophical foundation for believing that it makes sense. The myth-making has been presented with the assurance of a pseudo-science, convincing many that fanciful speculation is fact.

The nature of the UFO deception is such that as visions of strange lights and shapes in the skies become more common, they appear to bring with them proof of theories and beliefs about the universe that contradict Christian doctrine. If men can be convinced that the planet is being visited by extraterrestrials, then belief in evolution and a rejection of the teaching of Genesis is inevitable. In this confusion of ideas, we witness not a move to repentance and prayer, but to a willingness to embrace mystical traditions of the East as men seek to move deeper into the UFO experience.

Orthodoxy stands alone in its warning about UFOs. Both Roman Catholic and Protestant leaders have spoken warmly of alien visitors. This is to be expected, as Father Seraphim Rose explains:

The reason for this credulity is clear: Roman Catholicism and Protestantism, cut off for centuries now from the Orthodox doctrine and practice of spiritual life, have lost all capability for clear discernement in the realm of the spirits.(2)

Those currently attempting to examine the UFO phenomenon are not equipped to do so. It is something that can only be examined and understood from within the Orthodox Christian tradition. Those who attempt to apply scientific methods will only be further deceived; we already see this in the way some areas of scientific research have moved into occult practices such as telepathy and telekinesis.

Belief in UFOs also promotes the ideas of global unity, which may have a superficial attraction. However, those seeking to globalise their interests have shown their willingness to suppress cultural diversity and enforce a single ethical code: for example the European Union has repeatedly punished Poland and Hungary for their traditional stances on issues such as abortion and marriage. Like the threat of environmental disaster, anticipation of extraterrestrial attack may result in a move to the idea of a single humanity defending itself under a single world government. This threat has been explored in numerous publications. For the Orthodox Christian, the assurance is very clear. There is nothing to fear in this phenomenon, UFOs are merely a further manifestation of demonic presence. Our task is not to engage with them, or pursue them, it is to focus on the same spiritual struggles that the Church has always taught us. We are not in danger, UFOs cannot harm us, as long as we confess and repent of our sins, pray, receive Holy Communion, and trust in God's love. Satan is a liar and we must reject his deception.

Endnotes

1 – Saint Gregory the Great, Dialogues IV, p.251
2 – Rose, Seraphim, The Soul After Death, p.63